Every
Moment
a
Prayer

Emily Biggers &
JoAnne Simmons

Every Moment a Prayer

Devotional Inspiration
for Women

BARBOUR
PUBLISHING

Print ISBN 978-1-63609-302-4

Published by Barbour Publishing, Inc., 1810 Barbour Drive, Uhrichsville, Ohio 44683, www.barbourbooks.com

Our mission is to inspire the world with the life-changing message of the Bible.

Printed in China.

INTRODUCTION

Be cheerful no matter what; pray all the time;
thank God no matter what happens. This is the way
God wants you who belong to Christ Jesus to live.
1 THESSALONIANS 5:16–18 MSG

. . . .

These inspiring prayers will encourage you to celebrate a life of constant prayer.

Inspired by passages straight from God's Word, each turn of the page offers a beautiful starting point to your own daily prayer time. Touching on topics including joy, focus, rest, comfort, perseverance, wisdom, and more, you will be on your way to more meaningful, purposeful, honest conversation with your heavenly Creator.

Be blessed!

MY MOTIVES

You may believe you are doing right,
but the LORD judges your reasons.

PROVERBS 21:2 NCV

. . . .

God, You see my heart. You see more than appearances; You see motives. You are sovereign. . . . You see all and know all. There is no hiding my motives from You. Help me to be true to who I say I am in Christ. May my motives and desires reflect who You are. When others look at me, I want them to see a heart that passionately pursues Christ. I want to be known for being a Christ follower. Inspect my heart, God. I give You full rein. I love You, Lord, and I want so very much to look like You, so there is no doubt I am a daughter of the King. In Jesus' name, I pray. Amen.

SET FREE

Therefore, there is now no condemnation for those who are in Christ Jesus, because through Christ Jesus the law of the Spirit who gives life has set you free from the law of sin and death.

ROMANS 8:1–2 NIV

. . . .

Dear Father God, I imagine the slaves who were set free after the Civil War. How strange it must have felt to be imprisoned by a master one minute and set free as an independent human being the next! I have experienced a similar freeing through Christ. I once was bound by sin and darkness. My soul was bound for hell. There was no way I could come before You in all Your holiness. I was stained with sin so deep and dark that there was no chance for me. But when I invited Jesus into my heart, I was set free. All my sins were forgiven, and in just a moment's time, I passed from death to life. . .from sin to salvation. Lead and guide me all the days of my life, I pray. In the name of Your precious Son, Jesus, I pray. Amen.

LIVE AT PEACE

*If it is possible, as far as it depends on
you, live at peace with everyone.*
ROMANS 12:18 NIV

. . . .

Heavenly Father, I think the inability to live at peace with others comes down to selfishness. I get so caught up in myself sometimes that I am unable to see the bigger picture. Just because someone hurts me, I don't have to react in anger or retaliation. Just because I disagree, I don't have to argue or tear someone else down in order to promote my opinion. Just because I may be right, I don't have to push my agenda on others. There is a better way. It is the way Jesus showed us when He walked on earth. He came as a servant leader. He loved all people and walked humbly and in a godly manner. He modeled for me what it means to live at peace with people. When it is possible, please give me the humility and grace I need to live peacefully with those around me. In Jesus' name, I pray. Amen.

PRAISE TO THE GIVER

Anyone who belongs to Christ has become a new person. The old life is gone; a new life has begun! And all of this is a gift from God, who brought us back to himself through Christ. And God has given us this task of reconciling people to him. For God was in Christ, reconciling the world to himself, no longer counting people's sins against them. And he gave us this wonderful message of reconciliation.

2 CORINTHIANS 5:17–19 NLT

. . . .

Heavenly Father, I rejoice because You have given me this day. You are the Giver of life on earth and You are the Giver of eternal life in the kingdom You are preparing. I praise You for saving me from my sin. Thank You for reconciling me to You through Your Son, Jesus Christ. I want to know You and serve You better and better each new day. Amen.

LOVE ONE ANOTHER

No one has ever seen God; but if we love one another, God lives in us and his love is made complete in us.

1 JOHN 4:12 NIV

. . . .

Holy God, no one has ever seen You. You are too holy for us to look upon. And yet, I have seen You in others. I have seen You in teachers in my church who give of themselves tirelessly, serving and spreading Your Word to all who will listen. I have seen You in family members and friends whose hearts reflect compassion. They reach out instead of focusing inward. They reflect Your light in a dark world. Father, I pray that others would see that same light in me. As I work and play with friends and family, I pray that my love for them would be evident. I pray my words and actions would show that Jesus Christ has taken up residence in my heart and that I truly live for Him. I want to point others to You all my days, Father. In the name of Jesus, I ask these things. Amen.

A KIND WOMAN

A kindhearted woman gains honor, but
ruthless men gain only wealth.
PROVERBS 11:16 NIV

Kind God, give me a kind heart. Help me to commit random acts of kindness today that will bless my family and friends. When I am busy at work, help me to keep my cool and respond with grace and patience to others' demands. At the end of a long day, give me a gentle spirit as I deal with my family. Help me to listen and to nurture each member of my family with kindness, for I know this pleases You. You will replenish me with Your never-ending grace and love. You will continue to pour love into me so that I will have enough to pour it right back out into the lives of those who look to me as an example. I pray that I will never be known for what I have or what I earn, but rather for the kindness that spills forth from my heart. God, make me kind. In Jesus' name, I ask this. Amen.

NEAR TO GOD

*Come near to God and he will come near
to you. Wash your hands, you sinners, and
purify your hearts, you double-minded.*

JAMES 4:8 NIV

God, draw near to me. Just as I long for human
touch and connection, I long (even more so) for a
connection with You. You are my Creator, my Savior,
my very best Friend. Your Word tells me that when
I draw near to You, You are there. You have put in
me a free will. You have given me a choice. I can
choose to live life on my own, forgetting You are
there, neglecting Your Word, forging my own path.
Or I can depend upon You, draw from Your amazing
strength, and lean upon You. Father, I would be so
foolish to do anything but draw closer and closer
to You with each passing day. In times that I begin
to stray, reach out to me, Father. Never let me go.
I want to be in the safest place of all—in Your arms.
In Jesus' name. Amen.

REST IN THE LORD

Truly my soul finds rest in God;
my salvation comes from him.

PSALM 62:1 NIV

God, this world is busy. We find ways to occupy our every waking minute. Work dominates our days and nights. We busy ourselves with hobbies and meetings and even entertainment. We feel we must exercise and socialize. We work hard and play hard only to fall into bed at the end of long days without acknowledging You at all. Father, You are my only source of true rest. You offer me peace that this world does not know. The world may offer me many things, but peace it cannot give—the world knows nothing of peace. When my head hits the pillow tonight, may I be found faithful. May I seek You even in my rest. May I commit my soul to You even as I sleep. You are my Salvation and my Joy. You are my Strength and my Serenity. It is in the name of Your Son, Jesus the Christ, I pray. Amen.

ETERNAL IMPACT

We are always confident and know that as long as we are at home in the body we are away from the Lord. For we live by faith, not by sight. We are confident, I say, and would prefer to be away from the body and at home with the Lord. So we make it our goal to please him, whether we are at home in the body or away from it. For we must all appear before the judgment seat of Christ, so that each of us may receive what is due us for the things done while in the body, whether good or bad.

2 CORINTHIANS 5:6–10 NIV

Heavenly Father, please help me to remember every day that my actions here on earth have an impact on my eternal life. No matter my circumstances, I am Your child. I want to obey and please You through every blessing and through every trial. Today, please guide me in the good things You have planned for me, all for Your glory. Amen.

PROVISION

A hard worker has plenty of food, but a
person who chases fantasies has no sense.
PROVERBS 12:11 NLT

. . . .

Heavenly Father, You have always provided for me.
You meet my needs so wonderfully. The Bible says
that You even care for the birds of the air, providing
the food they need. . .and so how much more will You
provide for us—Your children! I ask You to keep me
grounded and focused on the work at hand. I have
seen what happens when people stray from that
focus and get caught up in chasing dreams. While
I know You can make dreams come true for me as
well, I want to thank You for the day-to-day routine.
Please bless me in my work each day, and help me
to honor You with not only my work but my attitude
about it as well. In Jesus' name, I pray. Amen.

A PRAYING CHURCH

*But while Peter was in prison, the church
prayed very earnestly for him.*

ACTS 12:5 NLT

. . . .

Help us, God, to be a praying church. It is easy in this day and age to think we can do things by our own strength. We have so much technology at our fingertips to make lights and music glorious. We have resources and money to do things within the walls of our church. We start planning classes and events and conferences; and sometimes, in the midst of all the good, we forget the best. You are all that matters. You are the Alpha and the Omega. The Beginning and the End. You are sovereign over all things. I pray that my church will find great peace in knowing that we are bathing every decision in prayer. Then we will know that we are on the right track and pleasing You, God. Remind us to pray earnestly for the body of Christ. It is in Jesus' name, I pray. Amen.

YOUR WILL FOR MY LIFE

Give me understanding and I will obey
your instructions; I will put them into
practice with all my heart.

PSALM 119:34 NLT

God, fill my thoughts with understanding. I know that when I can comprehend Your will for my life, I will follow gladly in Your ways. I want to please You with all my thoughts. I make a lot of plans for my own life, but I pray that I will always be attentive to the signs and factors that You use to direct me. I know that true peace and serenity will only be mine when I am led by Your hand. I want Your will for my life more than I want to go my own way. Father, give me an obedient heart. I will seek Your ways and listen to Your instructions. I will read Your Word to discover the truths You want me to live by. Help me to put Your ways into practice with all my heart. In Jesus' name, I pray. Amen.

THINK ON HEAVENLY THINGS

Think about the things of heaven, not the things of earth. For you died to this life, and your real life is hidden with Christ in God.

COLOSSIANS 3:2–3 NLT

- -

Heavenly Father, I know that this earth is not my home. I am but a visitor here, one who is passing through but who does not truly belong. My identity is in You. My old life has gone, and my new life is hidden with my Jesus in You. Help me to put any sinful ways to rest. I don't want death lurking where there should only be life. I don't desire the things of this world. But I do desire Your ways, Father, which are always higher and always best for Your children. Remove from my heart any fragment of greed or remnant of a past life of sin. I refuse to be a prisoner, even in my thoughts. I am free in Christ! I want my life to be a vessel of worship for You, my King. In Jesus' name, I pray. Amen.

EVERY REASON TO BELIEVE

Trust in the Lᴏʀᴅ with all your heart and lean not on your own understanding; in all your ways submit to him, and he will make your paths straight.

PROVERBS 3:5–6 NIV

. . . .

Heavenly Father, please refresh and renew my trust in You on this new day. You have proven Yourself time and time again, and I have every reason to believe You will continue to do so today and in the future. Strengthen my whole heart with great faith in You. I submit all my ways and all my mind to You, God. Please lead me along the straight paths You have laid out for me. Amen.

ANXIOUS FOR NOTHING

Do not be anxious about anything, but in every situation, by prayer and petition, with thanksgiving, present your requests to God. And the peace of God, which transcends all understanding, will guard your hearts and your minds in Christ Jesus.

PHILIPPIANS 4:6–7 NIV

. . . .

God, my emotions get the best of me sometimes. I let worry creep in and take over when I shouldn't. Remind me that You are always there, and You hear my prayers. Please help me not to let my emotions take control, but give me the presence of mind to take every thought captive to Christ. When I am under stress, I will take in a deep breath and let it out slowly. I will exhale, knowing that You have me in the palm of Your hand. You are bigger and greater than any fear or concern life may bring. You are my Peace Giver, my Delight, my Rest. I claim the power of Christ over my emotions, and I gladly surrender all my anxiety at the foot of Your throne. In Jesus' name, I pray. Amen.

JESUS WEPT

*When Jesus saw her weeping, and the Jews
who had come along with her also weeping,
he was deeply moved in spirit and troubled.
"Where have you laid him?" he asked. "Come
and see, Lord," they replied. Jesus wept.*

JOHN 11:33–35 NIV

· ·

Jesus, You wept. You were moved by the grief of others and by the death of Your beloved friend. You experienced real emotion. You were human, and yet God. You chose this place in all its sin; You chose earth—for me. You left heaven where there are no tears to come dwell here with us. You walked in our shoes. You hurt like we hurt. Thank You for that. Thank You for crying so I know You understand when I cry. Thank You for catching my tears and for comforting me, Father. You are good. You are *always* good. I love You, Lord. In Your powerful name, I pray. Amen.

IT IS WELL WITH MY SOUL

*Dear friend, I pray that you may enjoy good
health and that all may go well with you,
even as your soul is getting along well.*

3 JOHN 1:2 NIV

. . . .

Father God, my body and mind are connected. They
really can't be considered separately, because one
affects the other so greatly. Thank You that I have
found the secret to being at peace on the inside,
regardless of my outward circumstances. The apostle Paul wrote that he had learned to be content in
any circumstances, and I pray the same is true in
my life. I hope that no matter what happens, I will
maintain a wellness in my soul—a peace that is deep
and abiding—because I know I am Yours. I know You
are my God. I know that no matter what happens
in this life, I have the hope of heaven. Thank You,
Lord, that with Jesus in my heart I can truly say it is
well with my soul. In His name, I pray. Amen.

HEART FOCUS

Therefore we do not lose heart. Though outwardly we are wasting away, yet inwardly we are being renewed day by day. For our light and momentary troubles are achieving for us an eternal glory that far outweighs them all. So we fix our eyes not on what is seen, but on what is unseen, since what is seen is temporary, but what is unseen is eternal.

2 CORINTHIANS 4:16–18 NIV

Heavenly Father, sometimes I wake up with very little heart to face the day, but Your Word urges me to never lose heart. Remind me that even though everything in this fallen world—including me—is wasting away on the outside, You are renewing my eternal soul day by day. Please help me to keep my focus on the unseen things You are doing. Remind me how temporary this world and its troubles are, and fill me with joy and expectation for Your coming glory. Amen.

IN CHRIST'S STRENGTH

I can do all things through him who strengthens me.
PHILIPPIANS 4:13 ESV

. . . .

God, I have my strengths and weaknesses just like the next woman. But the Bible tells me that I can do all things through Christ, who strengthens me. *All things.* I think this means that anything I am called to do, I will have the strength to accomplish. If I am called to be a single woman, I can do it through Christ, who strengthens me. If I am called to be married, I can be a wife to my husband in Christ's strength. If You give me children, I can parent with the strength given to me by my Jesus. If I face hardships, I can walk through them because Jesus walks with me. He will guide me, assist me, and, at times, completely carry me through life. There is nothing that I cannot do because I have the power of Jesus Christ alive and well within my soul. I can do *all things* through my Jesus. It is in His name, I pray. Amen.

RESISTING PRIDE IN MY STRENGTHS

*Don't praise yourself. Let someone else
do it. Let the praise come from a stranger
and not from your own mouth.*

PROVERBS 27:2 NCV

. . . .

Heavenly Father, while I know it's good to be motivated and driven, please keep me from growing prideful. The gifts and abilities I have been blessed with are for Your glory, not mine. Allow me to use my gifts well and to learn and grow—not for self-glory but in honor of my King. I have heard it said that "pride goeth before a fall." I understand that praise should come from others and not from myself. I should be at work for an audience of one—You, my heavenly Father. I love You, Lord, and I thank You for the strengths You have bestowed upon me. Whatever I do, let me do it to the best of my ability—and not for the praise of men but in order to bring glory to You. In Jesus' name, I pray. Amen.

GOD PROTECTS ME

The LORD will protect you from all dangers; he will guard your life. The LORD will guard you as you come and go, both now and forever.

PSALM 121:7–8 NCV

. . . .

Lord, I am unsure about the future. I need Your reassurance that You are with me. You guard me and protect me because I am Yours. Everything may seem up in the air, but You have not lost sight of me. You keep watch over all my coming and going. Throughout the day and into the night, You sing over me, Father. You comfort me with Your presence. I am never alone. Even in the face of an unknown future, I will place my trust in You. You have never let me down before, and You aren't about to start! Thank You, Father, for Your steadfast love. Thank You for the promise that You will never let me go. In the name of Your Son, Jesus, I pray. Amen.

HEAVENLY PROTECTOR

*Those who live in the shelter of the Most High
will find rest in the shadow of the Almighty. This
I declare about the LORD: He alone is my refuge,
my place of safety; he is my God, and I trust him.
For he will rescue you from every trap and protect
you from deadly disease. He will cover you with
his feathers. He will shelter you with his wings. His
faithful promises are your armor and protection.*

PSALM 91:1-4 NLT

Heavenly Father, please remind me this new day
and every day that I live in the shelter of You, the
Most High. I find rest in Your shadow, Almighty One.
You are my Refuge and my Safety. You are my God,
and I trust You. You rescue me from every form of
evil in this world. You cover me and shelter me. I
am protected by Your faithful promises. Oh, how
grateful I am to be Your child! Amen.

AN EXTRAVAGANT GIFT

While Jesus was in Bethany in the home of Simon the Leper, a woman came to him with an alabaster jar of very expensive perfume, which she poured on his head as he was reclining at the table.

MATTHEW 26:6–7 NIV

. . . .

Dear Jesus, the disciples saw this woman's gift as a waste. She, who poured expensive perfume on Your head, was expressing her great love for You. She had saved the best for her Lord. And yet, she was scolded for her extravagant gift. But You told Your followers that she had done the right thing. How I hope I would have acted as the woman rather than as the disciples! How I hope that my best is always saved for my Master. How I hope that I never hesitate when there is a gift I possess that could be of use to You, Lord! Just as this woman poured perfume upon Your head, may I be prepared to give as I am led to do. In Your name, I pray. Amen.

COURAGE TO FACE CHANGE

"Be strong and courageous. Do not be afraid or terrified because of them, for the Lord your God goes with you; he will never leave you nor forsake you."

DEUTERONOMY 31:6 NIV

God, change is scary. I pray that I will find courage and strength to face the changes in my life. I need to sense Your nearness. As I step out of my comfort zone, I ask that You would provide a peace that passes all understanding. When I feel overwhelmed, I pray you would remind me that transitions require a lot from us. They take time to get used to. Soon I will look back on this change and be able to see the good in it. There are always blessings to be found. Help me to value the new and to loosen my grip on the old just a bit. I want to cherish the memories of what was, while at the same time embracing what has come to be. Thank You for change, Lord, and for walking through it with me. In Jesus' name, I pray. Amen.

HOPE IN THE LORD

Yet this I call to mind and therefore I have hope:
Because of the LORD's great love we are not
consumed, for his compassions never fail. They
are new every morning; great is your faithfulness.
LAMENTATIONS 3:21–23 NIV

Father God, You are faithful. Through all the changes I must endure, You remain. You hold on to me. You sing over me as I lay my head on my pillow and trust in You to see me through the night. I read that Your mercies are new every morning. I need them, God. I need to experience your mercies today—right now, God. I have been so self-reliant in the past, but right now I bow before You in submission. I realize that I can't get through this on my own strength. I need You every hour. Be gracious, Lord. See me through this change as only You can. In Jesus' name, I ask. . . knowing You will provide. Amen.

GOD IS WITH ME

"So do not fear, for I am with you; do not be dismayed, for I am your God. I will strengthen you and help you; I will uphold you with my righteous right hand."

ISAIAH 41:10 NIV

I am up against a challenge, Father. This is one of those times when I want to lean back into Your chest and listen to Your heartbeat. Like an earthly father who wants nothing more than to protect his children from harm, You long to protect me. You are my God. You have more strength than all the earthly fathers of this world combined. With You, I have no reason to fear. Strengthen me, I pray. Uphold me. Carry me into battle day by day until we are victorious and this challenge lies flat, like the giant Goliath from young David's perfect aim. It may loom large before me, but this challenge is child's play for You. Let's tackle it together. Bless me with peace and courage as we fight this, Lord. In Jesus' name, I pray. Amen.

PEACE IN THE FACE OF STRUGGLE

*"I have told you these things, so that
in me you may have peace. In this
world you will have trouble. But take
heart! I have overcome the world."*

JOHN 16:33 NIV

. . . .

Jesus, You are the Prince of Peace. And I need Your peace as I face this struggle. You told me that this world would have trouble. And right now it lies across my path like a boulder, and I have no idea how to move it. Whether You remove the trial or lead me through it, I ask for peace along the way. It may take days or weeks or even months. I may still be dealing with this challenge years from now. But I do know that day by day, I can walk in peace, even if this trouble doesn't disappear instantly. You are with me, and You are fully equipped to face the challenges ahead of us. Thank You for always being with me. I am so thankful we are in this together. In Your holy name, amen.

FINISH LINE

*Since we are surrounded by such a great cloud
of witnesses, let us throw off everything that
hinders and the sin that so easily entangles.
And let us run with perseverance the race
marked out for us, fixing our eyes on Jesus,
the pioneer and perfecter of faith.*

HEBREWS 12:1–2 NIV

Heavenly Father, just like I threw off the covers to
get out of bed this morning, help me to throw off
everything that keeps me from growing closer to
You. I want to rid my life of sin, which trips me up
and keeps me from doing the good things You have
planned for me. I want to run the race You have
marked for me and put all my focus on pleasing
You until I fall into Your loving arms at the finish
line. Amen.

THE LORD ANSWERS ME

When I was in trouble, I called to the
LORD, and he answered me.

PSALM 120:1 NCV

. . . .

Lord, I need You. Just as a little child calls out in the night when she is frightened, I call out to You now. You are right by my side the instant that I call to You. You are ready to help me face this giant. You have provided all the tools. I will put on the breastplate of righteousness; I will take up my shield; I will call to mind the promises of Your holy Word that give me assurance I will get through this. Every time I have faced trouble in the past, You have been there. I have erected altars of remembrance. There are so many of them! I am facing yet another battle now. Help me in this trial. Thank You for the peace I feel just knowing we are in this together. I know I never fight alone. In Jesus' name, I pray. Amen.

NOTHING SHALL SEPARATE ME FROM GOD

What then shall we say to these things? If God is for us, who can be against us? He who did not spare his own Son but gave him up for us all, how will he not also with him graciously give us all things? Who shall bring any charge against God's elect? It is God who justifies. Who is to condemn? Christ Jesus is the one who died—more than that, who was raised—who is at the right hand of God, who indeed is interceding for us. Who shall separate us from the love of Christ? Shall tribulation, or distress, or persecution, or famine, or nakedness, or danger, or sword?

ROMANS 8:31–35 ESV

- -

God, I am thankful for the peace I have in You. I am comforted when I read in Your Word that You will never leave me. If You are for me, it doesn't matter who else is against me. You are the God of the universe, and You are on my side. You are my Father. And You have good plans for me. Tribulation will not do me in. Distress is not my end game. I am a winner because I am on Your team. In Jesus' name, I pray. Amen.

GOD RESTORES THE YEARS EATEN BY LOCUSTS

"I will restore to you the years that the swarming locust has eaten, the hopper, the destroyer, and the cutter, my great army, which I sent among you."

JOEL 2:25 ESV

. . . .

God, I've wasted a lot of years. I was not who I should've been. I wasn't walking with You. It pains me to think of all that wasted time. Time I could have spent in Your Word. Time I could have spent serving You. I feel behind in my study of the Bible when I compare myself to others my age. I think of all those whom I could have led to Christ, but I was squandering away my time on useless pursuits instead. But You assure me that You will restore those years to me. With You, nothing is wasted. You are the Redeemer. You redeem my past. You use it. You set before me opportunities to share my testimony. God, You are the Restorer of wasted things. You bring beauty from ashes. In Jesus' name, I commit my past to You, asking You to redeem it. Amen.

LIVE IN THE PRESENT

The LORD says, "Forget what happened before, and do not think about the past."

ISAIAH 43:18 NCV

. . . .

Lord, I can't stop living in the past. I dig up old memories, and they drag me down. I heard once that if you live in the past, you will miss the present; and therefore, you will have no future. I think this is true. God, I want to enjoy today. You have placed blessings and opportunities in my life, and you want me to fully live. But I can't fully live until I lay down the past. Will You help me? I am Your child, and You are my Father. I trust that You will guide me. Show me the right people to talk to if I need godly counsel. Take me to the place of healing, whether it is through counseling or writing a letter to someone from my past. . .or whatever path You see fit. I love You, Father, and I thank You for helping me to find peace with my past. In Jesus' name, I pray. Amen.

LIGHT

Jesus spoke to the people once more and said,
"I am the light of the world. If you follow me,
you won't have to walk in darkness, because
you will have the light that leads to life."

JOHN 8:12 NLT

. . . .

Heavenly Father, the world seems to grow increasingly darker with sin, and that can feel so discouraging. Please remind me that You sent Your Son as the Light of the world. Jesus makes my path through this world clear, step by step, day by day. Your light leads to life, no matter how the darkness falls around me. Please help me to live in Your light and constantly shine it for others to see and follow You too. Amen.

MATURING IN FAITH

*When I was a child, I talked like a child, I thought
like a child, I reasoned like a child. When I
became a man, I stopped those childish ways.*
1 CORINTHIANS 13:11 NCV

Heavenly Father, You have prepared me for this
time. Each day I live is ordained by you. You decided
when I was to be born, and You led me to Jesus at
just the right time. You opened my eyes spiritually.
You saved me. As I live out this life, I pray that my
faith will grow. I am more mature in my walk with
You now than I was in the past. I pray that I will show
that maturity in the ways I serve You and reach out
to others. Show me opportunities to teach or lead
or use my spiritual gifts. I want to honor You in all I
do. I am ready to serve. Show me how You want to
use me, Lord. In Jesus' name, I pray. Amen.

THE DEAD IN CHRIST SHALL RISE

But we do not want you to be uninformed, brothers, about those who are asleep, that you may not grieve as others do who have no hope. For since we believe that Jesus died and rose again, even so, through Jesus, God will bring with him those who have fallen asleep. For this we declare to you by a word from the Lord, that we who are alive, who are left until the coming of the Lord, will not precede those who have fallen asleep. For the Lord himself will descend from heaven with a cry of command, with the voice of an archangel, and with the sound of the trumpet of God. And the dead in Christ will rise first. Then we who are alive, who are left, will be caught up together with them in the clouds to meet the Lord in the air, and so we will always be with the Lord.

1 THESSALONIANS 4:13–17 ESV

Heavenly Father, the promises in Your Word are clear. Heaven is real, and believers in Christ will spend eternity there. I trust that one day all believers will be reunited for a great big family reunion in the sky. And it will last for all eternity! In Jesus' name, I pray. Amen.

GOD CARES WHEN I GRIEVE

You have kept count of my tossings; put my tears in your bottle. Are they not in your book?

PSALM 56:8 ESV

. . . .

Abba Father, Daddy, You catch my tears. You save them in a bottle. You care. Each tear I cry hurts You. Your heart is a Father's heart, tender toward Your child. You do not wish to see Your daughter in anguish. I cry my eyes out, but in the end, I feel better. Tears sometimes help in a strange sort of way. They bring a release to my sorrow. They cleanse my soul and allow me to move forward. I think tears can be healthy at times. Thank You for creating emotions, Father. Keeping our feelings inside is never good. God, I love You and I thank You for caring for me. Help me to cast this grief at the foot of Your throne. Help me to trade my burden for Yours, which is lighter. I surrender my grief to You. In Jesus' name, I pray. Amen.

FAITH

Now faith is the assurance of things hoped for, the conviction of things not seen.

HEBREWS 11:1 ESV

. . . .

God, this world focuses on things that can be seen. Money, fashion, entertainment. The spiritual realm is much the opposite. I must learn to focus on what is unseen—this is faith. Faith is the assurance of things hoped for. It is a promise that there is more to this life than meets the eye. It is trusting that the sun will rise tomorrow if You will it to, Father. It is recognizing that I serve a God far bigger than myself, far grander than the boundaries of this world. You are able to work miracles. You are capable of far more than we can even imagine. Strengthen my faith, I pray. In times when I have only a tiny mustard seed of faith, I pray You would bless that offering of trust and grow it in Jesus' name. Amen.

MUSTARD SEED FAITH

He said to them, "Because of your little faith.
For truly, I say to you, if you have faith like
a grain of mustard seed, you will say to this
mountain, 'Move from here to there,' and it will
move, and nothing will be impossible for you."

MATTHEW 17:20 ESV

. . . .

God, I want to be like those listed in the Bible's roll call of faith. I want to be like Noah, who worked on the ark when he could not see the rain. I want to be like Abraham, who climbed the mountain, knife in hand, ready to sacrifice his beloved son if You asked him to. I want to please You with my faith the way the great men and women of the Bible did. I have but a mustard seed portion of faith to bring to You. I ask You to multiply it. You tell me in Your Word that I can do great things with even a small amount of faith. I ask You to make me a woman of greater faith. In Jesus' name, I pray. Amen.

GOD'S WORD GROWS MY FAITH

All Scripture is breathed out by God and profitable for teaching, for reproof, for correction, and for training in righteousness, that the man of God may be competent, equipped for every good work.

2 TIMOTHY 3:16–17 ESV

. . . .

God, thank You for Your Word. All scripture is breathed by You. I am confident that as I study Your Word, my faith will grow. I will be competent to serve You, using my gifts for Your glory. I am equipped for good works through the reading of Your Word. When I do these good deeds, others will see them. They will wonder what makes me tick. They will ask me why I care as I do, why I serve, why I minister to others in their times of need. The answer will always be simply, "Jesus." My good deeds can point others to Him. Bless me, Father, as I seek to grow in my faith. I want to honor You in my circumstances. Use me, I pray, in Jesus' name. Amen.

FAITH AND WORKS

But someone will say, "You have faith and I have works." Show me your faith apart from your works, and I will show you my faith by my works.

JAMES 2:18 ESV

. . . .

God, I show my faith through my works. The two go hand in hand. I cannot say I have faith and then just sit there and not do anything about it. Help me to never live in such a hypocritical manner. I find great peace when I am living out my faith. It requires something of me. It requires sacrifice. But it is a wonderful kind of tired when I grow tired from serving. Allow me to see the opportunities set before me to do good works. I will share my faith with those around me, and I will be faithful to You, Lord. Even when I am not faithful, You remain the same. Draw me close and teach me how to have more faith each day of my life. I love You. In Jesus' name, I pray. Amen.

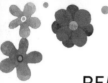

REMAIN FAITHFUL TO GOD REGARDLESS OF CIRCUMSTANCES

"If you throw us into the blazing furnace, the God we serve is able to save us from the furnace. He will save us from your power, O king. But even if God does not save us, we want you, O king, to know this: We will not serve your gods or worship the gold statue you have set up."

DANIEL 3:17-18 NCV

. . . .

Heavenly Father, Daniel and his friends were bold in negative circumstances. The king tried to get them to worship a gold statue instead of You, the one true God. He threatened to throw them into the blazing furnace. Even so, these men did not cower. They stood firm in their faith. They told the king that regardless of their circumstances, they would not bow to another god. They trusted You to save them from the fiery furnace, but they said that they would remain faithful to You even if You didn't. They would not let their circumstances dictate their faithfulness. Let it be so of me. In Jesus' name, I pray. Amen.

SERENITY IN SUFFERING

This is what you were called to do, because
Christ suffered for you and gave you an
example to follow. So you should do as he did.

1 PETER 2:21 NCV

. . . .

Jesus, You suffered. You were persecuted. You were betrayed. You hung on a cross between two thieves to die a painful death. You had done nothing wrong to deserve crucifixion and yet, You hung there for me. You suffered in my place. I will follow Your example. If suffering is God's will for me, I will try to endure it without complaining. I am not promised a carefree life. I am promised trouble in this life, because it is a fallen world since sin entered in. The good news is that You have overcome this world, Jesus. There is life beyond earth. There is hope beyond suffering. This is not the end but only the beginning. Allow me to suffer graciously. In Your precious name, I ask for serenity even in suffering. Amen.

LIKE A RIVER

Good leadership is a channel of water controlled by GOD; he directs it to whatever ends he chooses.

PROVERBS 21:1 MSG

. . . .

God, the future is very unclear to me. I take solace in the fact that You are in control. I want to be a channel of water controlled by You. Direct the flow. Lead me where You want me to go. Use me as You use a river, Lord. Use me to nourish and to strengthen others. Use me to help them move from one place to another. Use me to provide refreshment to their souls. God, channel me in the right way. Use my strengths and weaknesses and even my dreams in the way You can be glorified best. I want to be a leader who pleases You, one who is at Your disposal to do Your will all the days of my life. I hold loosely to any aspirations I may have, because the dreams You have for me are far greater than any human mind could conceive! In Jesus' name, I pray. Amen.

GOD CAN DO ANYTHING

*Now to him who is able to do far more
abundantly than all that we ask or think,
according to the power at work within us.*

EPHESIANS 3:20 ESV

. . . .

God, You have great plans for me. They are greater than my wildest dreams or my highest aspirations. Please help me to continue to work hard and set goals. Give me motivation to succeed and to grow. I have so many dreams for my life that I hope to see come true. But remind me that it is not "me, myself, and I" who make my dreams come true. It is all because of You. You know the plans You have for me, plans to bring me hope and a future. So if some of my dreams don't come true, help me to look for the silver lining in the cloud. Help me to look for Your purpose even in the times You say no instead of yes. In Jesus' name, I pray. Amen.

PRAYING FOR GOD'S WILL

"Your kingdom come, your will be done, on earth as it is in heaven."

MATTHEW 6:10 ESV

. . . .

Lord, Your name is holy, and Your ways are great. I come before You and pray as Jesus taught. I ask that You come quickly. This earth is not my home. But in the meantime, would You use me here? I want to be right in the center of Your will. I want to be Your good and faithful servant. I want my dreams to be Your dreams. What breaks Your heart should break mine. I want to carry out Your will on this earth, whatever that may mean. Reveal to me the needs in the world. Show me how my life can make a difference here. I love You, Father, and I am so thankful that I get to be a small part of what You want to do in this world. In Jesus' name, I pray for Your will to be done in my life. Amen.

CONTENT WITH MY APPEARANCE

"Has anyone by fussing in front of the mirror ever gotten taller by so much as an inch? All this time and money wasted on fashion—do you think it makes that much difference? Instead of looking at the fashions, walk out into the fields and look at the wildflowers. They never primp or shop, but have you ever seen color and design quite like it? The ten best-dressed men and women in the country look shabby alongside them."

MATTHEW 6:27–29 MSG

· ·

God, there is such order yet such creativity in all You have made. Such beauty. Such precision. Such forethought. There is no way that this world just appeared. It was designed by You, sovereign God. You are good. You created the trees in all their splendor, the mighty oceans white with foam, and the vast array of animal life. How could I ignore the fact that You also created me so beautifully? May I never waste time complaining about how I look. May I stop trying to improve upon what You made. In Jesus' name, I pray. Amen.

THE CHRISTIAN IS
NEVER ALONE

Turn to me and be gracious to me,
for I am lonely and afflicted.

PSALM 25:16 NIV

. . . .

Father God, I feel lonely. I need Your comfort and Your companionship. I love that because I am Your child, I never have to truly be alone. I have You near—always. You are at my side. You fight a spiritual battle for my soul in unseen realms. You keep me from falling into the devil's traps. You uphold me with Your righteous right hand. All the days of my life I will have a Friend. My Redeemer is not dead in the grave. He is very much alive. I think of those who worship idols. How sad it must be to pray to a statue rather than to a living being, a deity who came down to earth to become a man and dwell among His people. You are the one true God, and I am so thankful that I never have to be alone. In Jesus' name, I pray. Amen.

SUPERNATURAL REST

"Come to me, all you who are weary and burdened, and I will give you rest. Take my yoke upon you and learn from me, for I am gentle and humble in heart, and you will find rest for your souls. For my yoke is easy and my burden is light."

MATTHEW 11:28–30 NIV

. . . .

Heavenly Father, I come to You today weary and burdened, like Your Word describes. I desperately need You to give me the supernatural kind of rest only You can provide. Remind me that You don't want me to carry heavy burdens. Help me to give them up, Father. Please help me to focus only on the good things You want me to do. Align my priorities with Your will and Your ways. Amen.

PEACE IN WISDOM

Blessed is the one who finds wisdom, and the one who gets understanding, for the gain from her is better than gain from silver and her profit better than gold. She is more precious than jewels, and nothing you desire can compare with her. Long life is in her right hand; in her left hand are riches and honor. Her ways are ways of pleasantness, and all her paths are peace.

PROVERBS 3:13–17 ESV

. . . .

God, I know that it is better to find wisdom than to possess great riches. Nothing I desire compares with my desire for wisdom. I think, above all, I long for peace in my life. I have learned that there is sometimes peace even when I am not happy. The two do not necessarily go hand in hand. When I make a decision based on Your statutes and ways, I feel peaceful. I have honored You. Even if my choice was not popular in the world's eyes, even if I am misunderstood, I have peace. In Jesus' name, I pray. Amen.

CHRIST ALONE

See to it that no one takes you captive by philosophy and empty deceit, according to human tradition, according to the elemental spirits of the world, and not according to Christ.

COLOSSIANS 2:8 ESV

God, many people live by what their parents have taught them, whether it is right or wrong. They go along with traditions. They go through the motions of ceremonies and act as if it matters, when in the end, they are not changed at all on the inside. It is all outward. Just a show. Just a ritual repeated again and again. There is no wisdom in such activities. Father, may I always follow Christ and Christ alone. Let no one take me captive by philosophy or empty deceit. I do not wish to be entangled in human tradition or a new age movement. I will seek You and You alone. Please bless my life with wisdom and a calm assurance that is found only in following hard after Christ. It is in the name of Jesus, I ask these things. Amen.

FEAR OF THE LORD IS THE BEGINNING OF WISDOM

Give instruction to a wise man, and he will be still wiser; teach a righteous man, and he will increase in learning. The fear of the Lord is the beginning of wisdom, and the knowledge of the Holy One is insight. For by me your days will be multiplied, and years will be added to your life. If you are wise, you are wise for yourself; if you scoff, you alone will bear it.

PROVERBS 9:9–12 ESV

. . . .

Lord, You are a God of love, and I am Your beloved child. But I have a fear of You, just the same. It is a respect. It is a reverence. You are my heavenly Father. I come before You with respect. Please bless me with wisdom, God. I long to know You better. Give me insight as I read Your Word. Help me to read, not as one who wears spiritual blinders, but as one enlightened by my God. In Jesus' name, I ask these things. Amen.

A DAUGHTER OF THE KING

*Yet to all who did receive him, to those
who believed in his name, he gave the
right to become children of God.*

JOHN 1:12 NIV

Heavenly Father, thank You for adopting me into Your family. Thank You that I am truly a daughter of the King of kings. You call me Your heir, Your child, Your beloved daughter. I will walk with You all the days of my life. I don't wish to be known for my career or my wealth. I have no desire to be famous or strong or even popular. I want to be known for who I truly am—a believer in Christ—His apostle, His follower, His servant. As Your child, help me to walk in peaceful ways. Make me one who is patient and kind. Give me the ability, I pray, to identify others who need to know You. I want everyone I come in contact with to know what it means to be a child of God. In Jesus' name, I pray. Amen.

GREAT AND MIGHTY

Do you not know? Have you not heard? The Lord is the everlasting God, the Creator of the ends of the earth. He will not grow tired or weary, and his understanding no one can fathom. He gives strength to the weary and increases the power of the weak. Even youths grow tired and weary, and young men stumble and fall; but those who hope in the Lord will renew their strength. They will soar on wings like eagles; they will run and not grow weary, they will walk and not be faint.

ISAIAH 40:28–31 NIV

· ·

Heavenly Father, I so easily forget how great and mighty You are. Please forgive me, for there is nothing and no one comparable to You. I am blessed to be called Your child and privileged to serve You. As I begin a new day, fill me with absolute awe of You, my everlasting God. I give this day and every day of my life to You. All my hope and strength are in You. Amen.

A NEW CREATION

*Therefore, if anyone is in Christ, the new creation
has come: The old has gone, the new is here!*

2 CORINTHIANS 5:17 NIV

Heavenly Father, I thank You for the peace I find in knowing that I am a new creation in Jesus Christ! His death on the cross and my faith in Him has made me a brand-new person with a heart that has been cleansed from all unrighteousness. Though I continue to sin and mess up royally at times, You always stand ready to forgive. When You look at me, You see me not as a hopeless sinner but as a daughter of the King. I want to live today as a new being, one who has passed from death into life through the salvation provided by the blood of my Savior. Help me to please and honor You in all I do and say. I am more than enough in Your eyes because of the One who gave His all that I might be found sinless and blameless before You. It is in Jesus' name, I pray. Amen.

FROM DARKNESS TO LIGHT

As he neared Damascus on his journey, suddenly a light from heaven flashed around him.

ACTS 9:3 NIV

God, the story of Saul's conversion always inspires me. Saul was a persecutor of Christians. He was as far from You as anyone could imagine. And yet, You chose him. You shined a bright light down from heaven and appeared to him on the road to Damascus. In that moment, Saul's identity changed drastically. He believed in You, and his life was never again the same. Saul became Paul, the great apostle of the Lord Jesus Christ. He went from murderer to messenger in a flash. He laid down his weapons for the Word of God; he stopped killing and started evangelizing. I pray that others might see a difference in me, the way others saw a change in Saul. I want to be identified as one who walks closely with You, Lord. In Your Son's name, I pray. Amen.

LIVING FREE

*For we know that our old self was crucified with him
so that the body ruled by sin might be done away
with, that we should no longer be slaves to sin.*

ROMANS 6:6 NIV

God, I am no longer a slave to sin, but I have been set free. Help me to live as one who is free. Just as a dog that has been trained to sleep in a kennel will return to it night after night—even if the cage is not locked once he enters—I tend to wander back to my captivity. I remember what it was like to be a slave to sin. But then You entered my heart, and everything changed. My old self is no longer alive, so I never need wander back into slavery again. I am free, and I will live as if I am free indeed. Christ in me. Emmanuel. God with us. Remind me, every moment of every day, of the new identity You have blessed me with, Father. Help me to focus on Christ and never look back. In Jesus' name. Amen.

LOVE ONE ANOTHER

*"A new command I give you: Love one another.
As I have loved you, so you must love one
another. By this everyone will know that you
are my disciples, if you love one another."*

JOHN 13:34–35 NIV

. . . .

God of love, I am sorry that so many times my
words are not spoken in love. My actions are not
always a reflection of love either. My heart, at
times, is filled with anger or disgust and packed so
tightly with these emotions that there is no room
left for love. Help me to see others through Your
lens of love. Just as You have lavished love upon
me, may I in turn love them. I want to be known
as a child of God. I want the way I live and breathe
and act and serve to reflect Your great love for
the world. As I seek to live at peace with others,
will You help me to love them well? In Your Son's
name, I pray. Amen.

NO BETTER PURPOSE

*In a wealthy home some utensils are made of
gold and silver, and some are made of wood
and clay. The expensive utensils are used for
special occasions, and the cheap ones are for
everyday use. If you keep yourself pure, you
will be a special utensil for honorable use. Your
life will be clean, and you will be ready for the
Master to use you for every good work.*

2 TIMOTHY 2:20–21 NLT

Heavenly Father, You are my Master and I want to
be used for every good work You have for me. Help
me to keep myself pure, staying far away from sinful
actions, thoughts, words, influences, and attitudes.
I want my life to be clean and available to You so
that I can honor You and make You known! There
is no better purpose in life. I love You and long to
obey You. Amen.

BE OF ONE MIND

*Finally, brothers and sisters, rejoice! Strive
for full restoration, encourage one another,
be of one mind, live in peace. And the
God of love and peace will be with you.*

2 CORINTHIANS 13:11 NIV

• •

Father, I long for serenity in my relationships. I want
to be like-minded with those in my closest circles.
Before I look for the twig in my brother's or sister's
eye, allow me to see the log in my own, Father! May
there be a restoration of relationship in the broken
places You find in my life. Help me to be a peacemaker not a wave maker. Give me opportunities to
shine for You, and help me to be seen as one who
lives at peace with others. Replace my critical eyes
and tongue with vision and words straight from Your
holy heart. In Jesus' name, I pray. Amen.

GENEROSITY IN RELATIONSHIPS

A generous person will prosper; whoever refreshes others will be refreshed.

PROVERBS 11:25 NIV

. . . .

Heavenly Father, show me ways I can be more generous in my relationships. I know that, at times, I am too focused on my own problems. I share my latest complaint or concern with anyone who will listen! Calm my spirit, Lord, and help me to see—*truly see*—the needs of those around me. I experience such refreshment in the presence of certain friends. I literally leave my time with them feeling as though I have been in the presence of Jesus. Give me that type of generous and loving spirit so that I might be at peace in all my relationships. Even more, I pray that I am a blessing to all those with whom I come in contact. In Jesus' name, I pray. Amen.

BE FOUND TRUSTWORTHY

A gossip betrays a confidence, but a
trustworthy person keeps a secret.

PROVERBS 11:13 NIV

God, I know that being found trustworthy is of
extreme importance. I think of the great men and
women of the Bible who were upright and of good
character. They were not going around gossiping
about others. They were busy about Your work, and
they sought You through the reading of Your Word.
They came before You in prayer. They focused on
You and You alone. Teach me to concentrate fully on
doing Your will. Help me to be found trustworthy,
not only by others, but by You, my God. I want
to be someone whom others can trust. In Jesus'
name. Amen.

BE STILL AND KNOW

*He says, "Be still, and know that I
am God; I will be exalted among the
nations, I will be exalted in the earth."*

PSALM 46:10 NIV

Heavenly Father, as I enter into this quiet time
with You, I ask that You help me to remember You
are still God and You are still in control. You are
the Alpha and the Omega. Before there was time,
You were. If men and women do not praise You,
the rocks will have to cry out. You are that holy.
You are that supreme. You simply must be praised.
Father, help me to seek You and to truly find You in
my quiet times. As I still my heart before You and
open Your Word, lead me to the right scriptures
and the right messages from You. Clear my mind
of all the distractions that fight for my attention.
Help me to find peaceful moments alone with You,
in which You can encourage and strengthen me. I
need You so. In Jesus' name. Amen.

PEACE IN MY PRAYERS

*"But when you pray, go into your room,
close the door and pray to your Father,
who is unseen. Then your Father, who sees
what is done in secret, will reward you."*

MATTHEW 6:6 NIV

. . . .

God, I seek You here in private. Just the two of us.
I speak words of praise and thanksgiving. I present
requests to You for my own needs and the needs
of others. I ask Your forgiveness for sins—not just
in general, but for specific sins that come to mind
as I pray. I find time to be quiet before You here as
well. I do not desire to do all the talking. This is not
a one-way conversation. I cannot see You, Lord,
but I can feel You near me when I pray and when I
spend time in Your Word. Help me to always find
such peaceful, quiet times to withdraw from all the
responsibilities of the day and simply meet with my
Father. In Jesus' name, I pray. Amen.

NEVER DESPAIR

We are pressed on every side by troubles, but
we are not crushed. We are perplexed, but not
driven to despair. We are hunted down, but never
abandoned by God. We get knocked down, but we
are not destroyed. Through suffering, our bodies
continue to share in the death of Jesus so that
the life of Jesus may also be seen in our bodies.

2 CORINTHIANS 4:8–10 NLT

Heavenly Father, some days I feel like trouble is
coming into my life from every single direction.
When it threatens to completely overwhelm me,
remind me that You will never let it crush me or
destroy me or drive me to despair. You will never
abandon me in the midst of it. When I suffer, remind
me I share in the suffering of Your Son, Jesus. As
I depend on You for help with hardship, You make
Jesus' life and love known through me. Amen.

EARLY IN THE MORNING

*Very early in the morning, while it was still
dark, Jesus got up, left the house and went
off to a solitary place, where he prayed.*

MARK 1:35 NIV

Jesus, You set an example for me. I read in the book
of Mark that You went off alone to pray in a solitary
place. You went early in the morning. You didn't
wait until you fell into bed, exhausted, at the end
of a long day. You sought Your heavenly Father in
prayer first thing. This is the example You set for
me, and this is the example I will follow. I want to
honor You in all I do, including how I begin my day.
As I meet with You here and now, I ask You to calm
my spirit. Make this a time of tranquility. Enter into
my thoughts, I ask, and guide me with wisdom that
comes only from You. Put Your mark upon my day.
Thank You for this peaceful time with You. Amen.

FELLOWSHIP WITH GOD

"Here I am! I stand at the door and knock. If anyone hears my voice and opens the door, I will come in and eat with that person, and they with me."

REVELATION 3:20 NIV

• •

I am so blessed, Lord, that You have come into my life. I have the privilege of fellowshipping with the Creator of the universe. I get to visit with the great I Am. May I never take this privilege for granted or forget with whom I speak. You set the stars in their places. You know the number of hairs on my head. I am so blessed to be able to call out to You in prayer. It is only by the blood of Jesus that I am able to come before You. As I meet with You, as I sit at Your feet, Lord, I ask that You bring over me a sense of peace and joy. Regardless of outward circumstances, I can always find contentment in You, Father. It is in the name of the Prince of Peace, Jesus, that I pray this prayer. Amen.

FAITHFUL WORKER

Servants, do what you're told by your earthly masters. And don't just do the minimum that will get you by. Do your best. Work from the heart for your real Master, for God, confident that you'll get paid in full when you come into your inheritance. Keep in mind always that the ultimate Master you're serving is Christ. The sullen servant who does shoddy work will be held responsible. Being a follower of Jesus doesn't cover up bad work.

COLOSSIANS 3:22–25 MSG

God, I know that when I do my very best, others around me take notice. You tell me in Your Word to let my light shine before others so that they will see my good works and glorify my Father who is in heaven. This means that my work matters to You. Grant me the ability and desire to work as if I am working for You every single day. You are my ultimate authority, and I want to please You, Father. I know that when I am faithful in my work, You will show me favor. In Jesus' name, I pray. Amen.

WORK AND REST

By the seventh day God had finished his
work. On the seventh day he rested from all
his work. God blessed the seventh day. He
made it a Holy Day because on that day he
rested from his work, all the creating God had
done. This is the story of how it all started, of
Heaven and Earth when they were created.

GENESIS 2:2–4 MSG

Heavenly Father, I read in Ecclesiastes that there is a time for everything. A time to work and a time to rest. When You created the earth, You set a model for us to follow. You worked and then You rested. Grant me the wisdom in this, Lord. Help me to work hard and to please You in all that I do in the workplace. Help me also to know when it is time to rest. I need Your wisdom and guidance in order to strike a balance, Lord. May I always honor You in my work *and* in my rest. In Jesus' name, I pray. Amen.

HOUSEWORK

She carefully watches everything in her household and suffers nothing from laziness.

PROVERBS 31:27 NLT

. . . .

Father God, show me how to make the most of my time and to be organized in my approach to household tasks. Housework is not necessarily fun, but it is necessary, and I want to stay on top of it. I want my home to be a place of refuge and enjoyment for not only my family but for all who enter its doors. May I be blessed with Your favor as I seek to be the best woman that I can be. I need Your help, Lord, for I admit that working at home often feels so mundane and useless. Make me a faithful worker both inside and outside of my house. In Jesus' name, I pray. Amen.

WISDOM IN MY WORK

*She goes to inspect a field and buys it; with
her earnings she plants a vineyard.*

PROVERBS 31:16 NLT

. . . .

Heavenly Father, I am called on to make a lot of
decisions in my work. Every day there are choices
to be made, and I am not always sure what's best.
Give me wisdom, I pray, to make the best decisions.
Help me to always consider any ethical and moral
implications. Guide me to think about others and to
think beyond today and into the future. I read about
the wife and mother in Proverbs 31, and I see her
going about her work with precision and wisdom.
She inspects a field, buys it, and plants a vineyard.
She is not frivolous or flighty. She is busy at her
work, but she takes time to consider options and
she appears to take wise paths. Make me wise and
conscientious in all I do in my work. It is in Jesus'
name, I pray. Amen.

PERFECT PRAYER

"This, then, is how you should pray: 'Our Father in heaven, hallowed be your name, your kingdom come, your will be done, on earth as it is in heaven. Give us today our daily bread. And forgive us our debts, as we also have forgiven our debtors. And lead us not into temptation, but deliver us from the evil one.' "

MATTHEW 6:9-13 NIV

. . . .

Heavenly Father, I want to learn from the way Jesus taught us to pray. He honored and praised You. He longed for Your kingdom to come and Your will to be done on earth as it is in heaven. He asked for daily needs to be met. He taught us to seek forgiveness and to be willing to forgive others. He taught us to pray to avoid sin and temptation and to be delivered from evil. Please remind me of Your Son's perfect way of prayer every time I speak to You, dear Father. Amen.

AVOIDING SHORTCUTS

Good planning and hard work lead to prosperity,
but hasty shortcuts lead to poverty.

PROVERBS 21:5 NLT

God, a good attitude and hard work stand out in the world today. So many people are lazy or trying to find a way to make more money by doing less work. Even if it never gets me ahead or helps me climb the ladder of earthly success, I will be a success in Your eyes if I maintain a good work ethic. I don't want to be someone who is always looking for the next "get rich quick" scheme. Bless me, Lord, with discernment and skill so I can please You in my work all the days of my life. In Jesus' name, I pray. Amen.

PEACE IN MY WORK

*People who work hard sleep well, whether
they eat little or much. But the rich
seldom get a good night's sleep.*

ECCLESIASTES 5:12 NLT

• •

Thank You, heavenly Father, that I can lay my head
on my pillow at night and rest. Thank You for the
serenity that is found in simply putting in a good
day's work. Giving it my all. Staying the course.
Sticking to it when the going gets tough. Holding
my tongue and keeping my cool. Accomplishing
the tasks set before me day by day. I love You and I
thank You. I know that every good and perfect gift
comes down from the Father of lights. I know that
my job is a gift from You, and I pray I will always
remember to treat it as such. I ask that You would
help me to rest easy in the knowledge that I am
working hard and honoring my God. It is in Jesus'
name, I pray. Amen.

PEACE IN MY CHURCH

"Now I say to you that you are Peter (which means 'rock'), and upon this rock I will build my church, and all the powers of hell will not conquer it."

MATTHEW 16:18 NLT

Lord, Your Church has always been important to You, from the very start. You are our Good Shepherd; and when we gather together to worship You, You find it pleasing. I ask You, Jesus, to grant me serenity in my church. Help my church to be a place of peace. Help me not to sit back and hope things will improve, but help me to truly seek to be part of the solution. Where there is strife, help me to be a peacemaker. I thank You for my church, my pastor, our leaders, and the whole congregation. Each member is a blessing and is so special to You. Help us to see one another as You see us, Lord. Help us to value each other's opinions and ways. These things I ask humbly in Your powerful name. Amen.

CHURCH GROWTH

*So the churches were strengthened in
their faith and grew larger every day.*

ACTS 16:5 NLT

God, thank You for my church. I love the people
who gather there together in Your name. We have
become a family—the body of Christ in this community. There are people I can count on, and people
who can count on me. It feels good to belong, to
be a part of something bigger than myself. Help us,
Father, to grow—both in our faith and in numbers.
It isn't the numbers themselves that we seek, but
the souls that we know need to be saved by Jesus.
May we never grow so comfortable in who we are
as a body that we neglect reaching out beyond our
walls. I want my church to be a place where people
can come and feel welcomed. It should feel like a
welcoming family, ready to include all who enter in.
Bring growth to our church, Lord, and help me to be
a part of that growth. In Jesus' name, I pray. Amen.

THINK ON NOBLE THINGS

Finally, brothers and sisters, whatever is true, whatever is noble, whatever is right, whatever is pure, whatever is lovely, whatever is admirable—if anything is excellent or praiseworthy—think about such things.

PHILIPPIANS 4:8 NIV

Heavenly Father, I read in Your Word that You desire for me to think on noble things. Right things. That which is pure. That which is lovely, admirable, excellent, and praiseworthy. As I still my heart and mind before You, I ask that You would bring such things to my mind. Help me to focus on praising You. You are great and greatly to be praised. Bring to mind all that I have been blessed with so that I will be filled with a grateful heart. May I dwell on Your Word, which is truth and Your character, which is altogether lovely. May I think on things with substance and consequence—kingdom matters. In Jesus' name, I ask You to make my thoughts pleasing unto You, Father. Amen.

TRUTH, LIKE TREASURE

My child, never forget the things I have taught you. Store my commands in your heart. If you do this, you will live many years, and your life will be satisfying. Never let loyalty and kindness leave you! Tie them around your neck as a reminder. Write them deep within your heart.

PROVERBS 3:1–3 NLT

God, in the deepest parts of my soul, may I keep reminders of Your great love and all Your ways. You are my Father, and I, created in Your perfect image, want to love like You love and be faithful as You are faithful. You tell me that true satisfaction comes from remembering what You have taught me and living out Your will on this earth. Hold me close, Father, and whisper Your truth and Your love over me. In Jesus' name, I pray. Amen.

GOD'S VERY BEST

*We can rejoice, too, when we run into problems
and trials, for we know that they help us develop
endurance. And endurance develops strength
of character, and character strengthens our
confident hope of salvation. And this hope will
not lead to disappointment. For we know how
dearly God loves us, because he has given us
the Holy Spirit to fill our hearts with his love.*

ROMANS 5:3–5 NLT

· ·

Heavenly Father, too often life's trials make me
feel like giving up. Please assure me that You are
working in the middle of them to develop my character exactly as You have planned. I surrender to
You and the work You are doing in my life through
any kind of struggle and pain. I trust that You dearly
love me and are working out Your best for me in
all things. Amen.

DIRECT MY PATHS

*Trust in the LORD with all your heart; do not depend
on your own understanding. Seek his will in all
you do, and he will show you which path to take.*

PROVERBS 3:5–6 NLT

. . . .

Heavenly Father, I don't have the wisdom to know
even a fraction of what You know. You see my life
as a beautiful tapestry. You see all the threads and
colors woven together to create a wondrous picture. You see the beginning and the end. You see
everything in between. I see one little section at a
time. I need You to help me understand and follow
hard after You. This world calls out to me with many
voices. It seems that everywhere I turn, I have to
fight temptations to walk on paths I know lead to
nowhere. I want to walk on paths of righteousness.
I want to honor You, my God. In Jesus' name, I ask
for wisdom. Amen.

FOCUS ON GOD

Let your eyes look straight ahead; fix
your gaze directly before you.
PROVERBS 4:25 NIV

Heavenly Father, You tell me in Your Word not to look to the right or to the left but to look straight ahead. When I look around, I see so many things to worry about or to lead me off the right path. But when I look directly at You, I see nothing but Your glory. I am filled with a sense of calm. I am secure in my Father's care. I know that You are my Guide and my Provider. Just as little sheep depend upon the sound of their shepherd's voice, I depend upon You to direct me. Keep me always focused on You. In Jesus' name, I pray. Amen.

TAKE EVERY
THOUGHT CAPTIVE

We demolish arguments and every pretension
that sets itself up against the knowledge
of God, and we take captive every thought
to make it obedient to Christ.

2 CORINTHIANS 10:5 NIV

God, I will choose today to take every thought captive to my Jesus. I know that as my thought life goes, so goes my spiritual life. Please don't let my thoughts lead me to unholy places. Keep me from conflict and arguments. Keep me from sin, I pray. As soon as a thought begins to creep into my mind that may not be a righteous thought, may I recognize it and take it captive to Christ. Clear my mind now as I come before You in prayer and in surrender. Help me to truly turn over my thoughts to You. In Jesus' name, I ask these things. Amen.

NOT LETTING EMOTIONS RULE OVER ME

A happy heart makes the face cheerful,
but heartache crushes the spirit.

PROVERBS 15:13 NIV

. . . .

God, I have heard it said that attitude is a little thing that makes a big difference, and I believe that to be true. When I allow circumstances to dictate my emotions, I quickly go down a road that leads to depression and sadness. But when I, instead, choose to look on the bright side, my heart is lifted and my whole self follows. Bring a peace that passes all understanding to my heart, I pray. A peace that this world cannot offer. A peace that is available only to the believer, only to the one whose trust is in You. I pray that I will learn to count even the trials as joy, knowing that trials develop character in me and make me more like Jesus. It is in His name I pray this prayer. Amen.

THE COMFORT OF
THE HOLY SPIRIT

*"Blessed are those who mourn, for
they will be comforted."*

MATTHEW 5:4 NIV

Lord, You have told me You have gone to heaven to prepare a place for me so that I might spend eternity with You. You have left the Holy Spirit in Your place, and one of His main jobs is to serve as the Comforter. This brings me a lot of peace, knowing that You predicted I would need such help. When You ascended into heaven, You thought of me. You saw into my future. You saw the grief, and You didn't want me to cry alone. You wanted me to have a Comforter. Thank You for that, Jesus. Thank You for the sweet comfort of Your Holy Spirit that I sense near me even now. In Your name, I pray. Amen.

SEEK PEACE
AND PURSUE IT

*Turn from evil and do good; seek
peace and pursue it.*

PSALM 34:14 NIV

. . . .

Heavenly Father, my emotions can lead me astray—
and quickly! When I am sad or angry, I can easily go
down the wrong road. I start condemning myself
or others, creating burdens that we are not meant
to bear. I say things I don't mean. I act in a manner
that does not reflect the Gospel of Christ. Help
me in these moments to stop and simply turn to
You. Help me to seek peace and to chase after it.
If I lose a friendship because someone is just too
conflict prone over an extended period of time,
then teach me to cut my losses. There may be a
price to pay for peace sometimes. I pray that I
would be a pursuer of peace and serenity and that
I would not dishonor you because of emotions that
have run wild and taken me off course. In Jesus'
name, I pray for control over my emotions. I pray
for peace. Amen.

DRAW CLOSE

I urge you, first of all, to pray for all people. Ask God to help them; intercede on their behalf, and give thanks for them. Pray this way for kings and all who are in authority so that we can live peaceful and quiet lives marked by godliness and dignity. This is good and pleases God our Savior, who wants everyone to be saved and to understand the truth. For, There is one God and one Mediator who can reconcile God and humanity—the man Christ Jesus. He gave his life to purchase freedom for everyone.

1 TIMOTHY 2:1–6 NLT

. . . .

Heavenly Father, I know many people who are not in relationship with You through the Mediator You sent us, Jesus Christ. Please help these dear people with all their needs, and draw them close to You. I pray they come to believe in Your Son as the one and only Way, Truth, and Life. I pray they accept Jesus Christ as the Savior of their sins and their only hope for eternal life. Thank You for the privilege of knowing and praying for these people. Amen.

ONE SPIRIT

So then, let us aim for harmony in the church and try to build each other up.

ROMANS 14:19 NLT

. . . .

Heavenly Father, I love the word *harmony*. Please bless my church always with peace and tranquility. The world seeks to tear us down, but Your Church is a place where we can build one another up instead. Give us Your eyes to see one another as precious and cherished. May we always be a church that is known for our love, Lord. Bless us with a deep, abiding love for You as our sovereign Lord and for one another in the body of Christ. Help us to love the foreigner and the stranger well. Help us to be a place of peace for those who are hurting. Help us to be a refuge for the weary. Your Church is, in a sense, a hospital. May we minister to those who are wounded and encourage them in the faith. It is in Jesus' name, I ask for harmony in my church. Amen.

SELF-CONTROL

*God did not give us a spirit that makes us afraid
but a spirit of power and love and self-control.*

2 TIMOTHY 1:7 NCV

. . . .

Dear God, I have been given a spirit of power, love, and self-control. I have power over my emotions in the name of Jesus. I can control how I react when I am tapped into Your power source. I find that if I'm not spending time in the Word and in prayer, I am less likely to respond calmly when I'm hit with a stressful situation. Thank You that You have put Your power in me. The same power that raised Jesus from the dead lives inside of me; and through that power, I am more than a conqueror. Thank You, Father! In Jesus' name, I pray. Amen.

IN HIS IMAGE

So God created man in his own image,
in the image of God he created him;
male and female he created them.

GENESIS 1:27 ESV

Father God, You made everything in the world, but Your final masterpiece was mankind. You were not satisfied with Your created world until You placed man and woman in the garden. I am their descendent. I bear Your image, just as they did. When I look in the mirror, I see my weaknesses. They go far deeper than my outward appearance. I realize I am so very limited. I fail You every day, Father. I want to be perfect. I want to do things well and to be smart and attractive and. . .enough. I admit I struggle with wanting to be *enough.* But I hear You whisper to me, *"Daughter, you are enough."* Thank You, Father, for making me in Your image and saving me through Your Son. I am Your precious daughter. What a blessing, God. In Jesus' name, I pray. Amen.

POWER IN WEAKNESS

He gives strength to those who are tired
and more power to those who are weak.

ISAIAH 40:29 NCV

God of all power, when I am weak, You are strong. What a blessing to know that I am not expected to or required to be the best at everything. There will always be areas of my life in which I am weak. I may be good at hospitality but not gifted in teaching children's Sunday school. I may be a wonderful behind-the-scenes helper, but being in charge of a ministry may scare me to death! I am not created with all the spiritual gifts, but the ones I have I am responsible for using for Your kingdom. And when I am called upon to do something that takes me way out of my comfort zone, I need not fear. You are with me, and You will forever be my power source. I can tap into the power available to me through Christ anytime and in any place. I surrender my weaknesses to You, Lord, for in You I am strong. In Jesus' name, I pray. Amen.

BEARING FRUIT

"I am the vine, and you are the branches. If any remain in me and I remain in them, they produce much fruit. But without me they can do nothing."

JOHN 15:5 NCV

Heavenly Father, I need You every moment of every hour in order to bear fruit. And so I must abide in You. Keep me close to Your side, Father. Never let me stray. As I spend time in Your scriptures, dwelling upon and meditating on Your words, I abide in You. As I sit still and pray, giving You time to speak to me, I abide in You. And as I abide in You, I will bear more and more fruit for Your kingdom. Without You, I can do nothing; but through the power of Your Spirit, I am able to shine for the kingdom. In Jesus name, I ask that I would always abide in You and that I would bear much fruit. Someday, I want to hear these words: *"Well done, good and faithful servant. Well done."* Amen.

WISDOM FOR LIFE

If you need wisdom, ask our generous God, and he will give it to you. He will not rebuke you for asking. But when you ask him, be sure that your faith is in God alone. Do not waver, for a person with divided loyalty is as unsettled as a wave of the sea that is blown and tossed by the wind. Such people should not expect to receive anything from the Lord. Their loyalty is divided between God and the world, and they are unstable in everything they do.

JAMES 1:5–8 NLT

Heavenly Father, I need Your wisdom in every area of my life. You promise in Your Word to give it, and I believe You. Help me to apply the wisdom You are giving to the challenging situations I'm in the middle of and the tough decisions I need to make—and simply in my day-to-day life as I strive to serve and glorify You. Help me to point others to You and Your perfect wisdom too. Amen.

WORK VS. REST

"Come to me, all of you who are tired and have heavy loads, and I will give you rest. Accept my teachings and learn from me, because I am gentle and humble in spirit, and you will find rest for your lives."

MATTHEW 11:28–29 NCV

. . . .

Sometimes, Father, I grow weary. I work and strive and try to accomplish so much. I often wear myself out. I know exhaustion isn't Your plan for me. Help me to strike the right balance between serving and resting, between using my gifts and simply finding solace in Your presence. Just as Mary and Martha, the two sisters, struggled over what was best—sitting at Your feet or working to serve You— I find the same question relevant in my own life. Calm my spirit. Show me when to work and when to rest. Remind me that You are here to bear my heavy load and that when it all just gets to be too much, I am free to say no to some things. I am free to rest in Your presence. In Jesus' name, I pray. Amen.

FOCUS ON THE PRESENT

"Give your entire attention to what God is doing right now, and don't get worked up about what may or may not happen tomorrow. God will help you deal with whatever hard things come up when the time comes."

MATTHEW 6:34 MSG

Heavenly Father, I worry too much. I don't want to live with a sense of dread but with a lightness in my step. I am a believer in Jesus; He has made me new. My old life has gone, and my new life should reflect an inner trust and peace in knowing Him. Father God, hard things will come. This is a fallen world in which we live, and I am promised that there will be trials and tribulations. But You will see me through those troubles one step at a time. Remind me to enjoy the moment, God. Remind me to savor the serenity of walking through life with a Savior who will never leave or forsake me. There is great peace in trusting Jesus with my future. In His name, I pray. Amen.

DON'T WORRY

"Don't worry and say, 'What will we eat?' or 'What will we drink?' or 'What will we wear?' The people who don't know God keep trying to get these things, and your Father in heaven knows you need them. Seek first God's kingdom and what God wants. Then all your other needs will be met as well. So don't worry about tomorrow, because tomorrow will have its own worries. Each day has enough trouble of its own."

MATTHEW 6:31–34 NCV

. . . .

God, I have been told that tomorrow has enough trouble of its own. I shouldn't borrow trouble. Remind me again of this truth. You will provide what I need when I need it, just as You always have in the past. You know my needs even before I do. And You have not brought me this far to leave me high and dry! You are so strong. You are so good. You are with me and for me, and You never leave. Stay with me now, Lord. Comfort me. I need to sense Your presence. In Jesus' name, I pray. Amen.

THE PLANS GOD
HAS FOR ME

*"For I know the plans I have for you," declares
the LORD, "plans to prosper you and not to harm
you, plans to give you hope and a future."*

JEREMIAH 29:11 NIV

. . . .

Lord, You know the plans You have for me. You see
the future even though it is so unclear to me. I
stand here very uncertain of what tomorrow holds,
but You are never uncertain. You are my Creator
and my Sustainer. You are the great I Am. You are
what I need in every moment. You are my King of
Glory and my Prince of Peace. You are the Bread of
Life that sustains me. You are manna from heaven,
day by day. You meet my needs and show me just
a few steps ahead at a time. You do not reveal to
me more than I can handle. You shine Your light
on my next step, and I take it in faith that You will
direct me when it is time to step out again. I find
great serenity in knowing You go before me. I love
You, Lord. In Jesus' name, I pray. Amen.

WORRIES TURNED INTO PRAYERS

"I tell you, do not worry about your life, what you will eat or drink; or about your body, what you will wear. Is not life more than food, and the body more than clothes? Look at the birds of the air; they do not sow or reap or store away in barns, and yet your heavenly Father feeds them. Are you not much more valuable than they? Can any one of you by worrying add a single hour to your life?"

MATTHEW 6:25–27 NIV

. . . .

Heavenly Father, Your Word tells me not to worry, but I still struggle with it far too often. Please help me to turn each worry that pops into my mind into a prayer instead, remembering You are sovereign and good and are working in every situation and need. When worries threaten to consume me, please fix my thoughts on trusting and praising You. There is absolutely nothing You cannot handle. Amen.

GOD IS WITH ME

*"The Lord your God is with you, the Mighty
Warrior who saves. He will take great delight
in you; in his love he will no longer rebuke
you, but will rejoice over you with singing."*

ZEPHANIAH 3:17 NIV

. . . .

Heavenly Father, I find peace when I read in Zephaniah that You will rejoice over me with singing. That is such a wonderful promise! As I feel myself beginning to fear the future and all of life's uncertainty, I fix my eyes again on Jesus. I see Him there on the cross, dying for my sin. That kind of love is beautifully unfathomable. It is not found in golden calves. It is not offered by Allah or Mohammad. It is not available in the Buddhist temple or in the mosque. It comes only from the one true God. I reach out to You now, in faith, in the face of a very uncertain future. And I cling to my very certain God. In Jesus' name, I pray. Amen.

GOD HAS GREAT PLANS FOR ME

However, as it is written: "What no eye has seen, what no ear has heard, and what no human mind has conceived"—the things God has prepared for those who love him.

1 CORINTHIANS 2:9 NIV

Father God, when I look at Your universe, I see Your handiwork. I see it on display in the magnificent sunsets and the glorious sunrises. You paint rainbows in the sky. You have dotted the earth with rushing waterfalls and creatively designed animals of all kinds. You have a wild imagination, Father! To think that You have such wonderful and wild plans for me! . . . I can rest easy, remembering that the future—my future—is in Your capable hands. In Jesus' name, I pray. Amen.

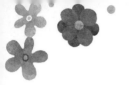

PROTECTION FROM GREED

For the love of money is a root of all kinds of evil.
Some people, eager for money, have wandered from
the faith and pierced themselves with many griefs.

1 TIMOTHY 6:10 NIV

Heavenly Father, thank You for blessing me financially. Thank You for my job and for the ability to pay my bills. Help me to always see money as merely a resource and not a treasure to be hoarded. I want to use all my resources, including my financial resources, for Your kingdom. When I see a need, I want to be free to meet it. Lord, show me opportunities to bless others. Thank You for my church and the blessing of tithing. Through my church, I know that my financial gifts are being used responsibly. I pray that You would always bless this area of my life and remind me to be generous with the resources You give me. Please protect me always from the love of money, which is the root of many evils. I ask this in Jesus' name. Amen.

THE LOVE OF MONEY

Whoever loves money never has enough;
whoever loves wealth is never satisfied with
their income. This too is meaningless.

ECCLESIASTES 5:10 NIV

- -

God, I love You. I love Your world and Your people. I love sunsets and sunrises painted by Your hands—masterpieces for Your children to enjoy. I love Your Word, full of wisdom and truth, which teaches and corrects me every day of my life. I love Jesus, who died upon the cross for my sins. I love my family and my friends, people hand-chosen by You to enrich my life. I love the seasons of the year and how they remind me that You are always in control and that You are a God of order. But I do not love money—which is nothing but a resource, a tool. Help me to always to be content and thankful for whatever money You bestow upon me. And help me to use it wisely. In Jesus' name, I pray. Amen.

GIFTS

Jesus sat down near the collection box in the Temple and watched as the crowds dropped in their money. Many rich people put in large amounts. Then a poor widow came and dropped in two small coins. Jesus called his disciples to him and said, "I tell you the truth, this poor widow has given more than all the others who are making contributions. For they gave a tiny part of their surplus, but she, poor as she is, has given everything she had to live on."

MARK 12:41–44 NLT

Heavenly Father, sometimes I feel like I don't have much to offer You, especially when I take my eyes off You and spend too much time comparing myself to others. Forgive me. Every single gift I have—whether it is a quality or talent, money or a material possession—ultimately comes from You. So no matter how big or small my gifts seem, I offer everything back for Your use—to build Your kingdom, to share Your truth and love, and to give You all the glory. I know You can multiply anything I give into so much more. Amen.

SERVE GOD, NOT MONEY

"No one can serve two masters. Either you will
hate the one and love the other, or you will
be devoted to the one and despise the other.
You cannot serve both God and money."

MATTHEW 6:24 NIV

. . . .

Heavenly Father, You are my Master and my Lord. I want to follow in Your footsteps and walk in Your ways. I see those who chase after money. They have made money their god. They worship it and seek it. They devour it when they find it. And, for them, there is never enough. There is no end to the vicious cycle. When times are good and money is abundant, they are happy. When times are bad and the money is scarce, they fall into depression. If a person's whole world is built upon a foundation of cash and coins, it is certain to crumble. Thank You for Your provision of the money that I need to support my family. Thank You for the deep peace I find in knowing that You are my God and that money is merely a tool You provide. In Jesus' name, I pray. Amen.

DEBT-FREE LIVING

Let no debt remain outstanding, except the continuing debt to love one another, for whoever loves others has fulfilled the law.

ROMANS 13:8 NIV

Heavenly Father, I haven't always been wise with money. I pray that You will guide me and show me ways to allocate my money so that I can pay off debt. I truly want to be debt free so that I may honor You in this area of my life. I know that when I rid myself of debt, I will be opening up my world to a new level of peace. All the time I spend worrying about money I can then devote to serving You and showing love to those around me. I will have more money to give to good causes. I will be able to support Your Church better. I pray for guidance that I might get out of debt quickly. Thank You, Father, for hearing my prayer. I know You will help me. In Jesus' name, I pray. Amen.

JESUS NEVER CHANGES

*Jesus Christ is the same yesterday
and today and forever.*
HEBREWS 13:8 NIV

. . . .

Jesus, You are always the same. You have not changed. When everything around me is altered, You remain. You are steadfast. The same yesterday, today, and tomorrow. You are good. You are above all things and before all things. You hold all things together. Help me to dwell on these truths and to rest in You. In times of insecurity, may I cling to You, my Rock and my Redeemer. You are a mighty Fortress. Thank You for helping me to know and understand that You will never change and You will never leave me. I find such comfort in this! I can rest easy in the knowledge that You are still here and You are forever by my side. I surrender all to You, Jesus. This change. This uncertainty. This worry. Help me to adjust well, Lord. Help me to release control to You. You are more than capable of handling this for me! In Your name, I pray. Amen.

GOD MAKES A WAY

*"See, I am doing a new thing! Now it springs up;
do you not perceive it? I am making a way in
the wilderness and streams in the wasteland."*

ISAIAH 43:19 NIV

. . . .

Lord, you are a God of the unexpected. You bring about changes we don't count on but that are just right for us. You know us individually. You understand our strengths and weaknesses. You see our needs. You make a way where, frankly, at times there seems to be no way. You create a stream in the wastelands. You clear a path through the wilderness. Although this is uncharted territory for me, You have been here already. You have made Your preparations for me to come to this place in life. You know me, and You know all about this change that has come along. I will walk with You, Father. I will hold on to Your strong hand and let You guide me through this land. Thank You, God, for always looking out for me. In the name of Christ, I pray. Amen.

DO NOT LOSE HEART

Therefore we do not lose heart. Though outwardly we are wasting away, yet inwardly we are being renewed day by day. For our light and momentary troubles are achieving for us an eternal glory that far outweighs them all. So we fix our eyes not on what is seen, but on what is unseen, since what is seen is temporary, but what is unseen is eternal.

2 CORINTHIANS 4:16–18 NIV

Renew me day by day, Lord. Sometimes I need Your renewal more often—hour by hour, even moment by moment. I know You are able to help me. I know my struggle is temporary. In time, it will pass. And this change, this transition, this "new" that replaces the familiar—it has a purpose. I can trust that You are not going to waste it in my life. You will use it for my good. Help me not to look at the problem, but rather to look up. Help me to focus on Jesus, who is the same yesterday, today, and forever. In His name, I pray. Amen.

INNER STRENGTH

When I think of all this, I fall to my knees and pray to the Father, the Creator of everything in heaven and on earth. I pray that from his glorious, unlimited resources he will empower you with inner strength through his Spirit. Then Christ will make his home in your hearts as you trust in him. Your roots will grow down into God's love and keep you strong. And may you have the power to understand, as all God's people should, how wide, how long, how high, and how deep his love is.

EPHESIANS 3:14–18 NLT

. . . .

Heavenly Father, I pray that from Your glorious, unlimited resources You will empower me with inner strength through Your Spirit. I want Christ to be comfortably at home in my heart as I trust in Him. I want strong roots growing down deep into Your incredible love for me. I cannot ever fully understand it here on earth, but every day I want to understand more and more of how wide, long, high, and deep Your love is. What an unfathomable honor and blessing it is to be Your child! Amen.

BLESSINGS IN CHANGE

"For my thoughts are not your thoughts, neither are your ways my ways, declares the LORD. For as the heavens are higher than the earth, so are my ways higher than your ways and my thoughts than your thoughts."

ISAIAH 55:8–9 ESV

. . . .

God, I find myself on a brand-new path. These surroundings are strange to me. The winds of change have taken me to a new place with a new purpose; and honestly, I feel lost. Thank You that You are still on the throne. You are still in control. You have plans for me. And You will bring good from this transition. This change may not be comfortable or easy or even welcomed, but it is going to be okay. Because You are my God, and I trust in Your ways. Your understanding is far greater than mine. In Jesus' name, I commit this change to You. In His name, I pray. Amen.

FOCUSED ON THE LORD

*I keep my eyes always on the LORD. With him
at my right hand, I will not be shaken.*

PSALM 16:8 NIV

. . . .

Jesus, I remember the story of Your disciple who
set out to walk upon the water. As long as he kept
his eyes on You, he walked across the surface of
the sea. But when he lost his focus, he began to
sink. When I stare into the face of this trial, it is
too much for me to bear. I cower at its immense-
ness. But then You appear, Jesus. You reach out
to me. You remind me to hold strong to my faith.
You assure me that if You could make a man walk
upon water, You can smooth this path out before
me—and You will. It may take time. But together,
we can conquer this. I will keep my eyes on You. I
refuse to let Satan win. I will not be shaken. I will
rely on You, my Savior, and in Your strength, I will
prevail. In Your name, I pray. Amen.

CASTING MY CARES ON HIM

Cast your cares on the LORD and he will sustain you; he will never let the righteous be shaken.

PSALM 55:22 NIV

. . . .

Lord, I give You my cares and concerns. I offer this challenge to You as a sacrifice on the altar. I need You to sustain me. I need You to uphold me. I am weary from the struggle; I have no more strength. I am through trying to face this on my own. Will You fight the battle in my place? Will You go before me? Will You defend me on all sides? Will You bring me success? I trust You to see me through, as only You can do. I have struck out on my own enough. I should have learned by now that some trials are just too tough for a mere human. There are battles waging for my soul in the spiritual realms. And this is one of them. Fight for me, Jesus. I trust in You. Amen.

HELP FROM THE LORD

If you don't know what you're doing, pray to the Father. He loves to help. You'll get his help, and won't be condescended to when you ask for it. Ask boldly, believingly, without a second thought. People who "worry their prayers" are like wind-whipped waves. Don't think you're going to get anything from the Master that way, adrift at sea, keeping all your options open.

JAMES 1:5–8 MSG

. . . .

I don't know what I'm doing, Lord. I come before You confidently, not sheepishly. I am not a stranger to You. I am Your child. I am requesting the aid of my Creator, my Father, my Redeemer, my best Friend. You are my Abba Father, my Daddy. You are the One who knows me and sees me. You know the way out of this mess I have gotten myself entangled in, and I need You to work. Boldly, I pray for Your assistance. I thank You in advance, because I know that help is on the way. In Jesus' name, I pray. Amen.

ALL THINGS WORK TOGETHER FOR GOOD

And we know that in all things God works for the good of those who love him, who have been called according to his purpose.

ROMANS 8:28 NIV

* *

Heavenly Father, remind me today that *all things* work together for good in the lives of those who love You. This includes my disappointments and my failures. It means that there is not a mistake that You cannot redeem in my life for Your purposes. You are bigger than my mistakes. You are bigger than my dreams that don't come true. You take the broken pieces and the fragments that are left, and You put them together to create a beautiful masterpiece. It may be different than the one I had imagined, but it will be even better! You are a good God, and You have good plans for me. You are using all things together for my good. Thank You for that, Lord. It brings me peace in the midst of disappointment. In Jesus' name, I pray. Amen.

AMAZING GRACE

Come, my children, and listen to me, and I will teach you to fear the LORD. Does anyone want to live a life that is long and prosperous? Then keep your tongue from speaking evil and your lips from telling lies! Turn away from evil and do good. Search for peace, and work to maintain it. The eyes of the LORD watch over those who do right; his ears are open to their cries for help. But the LORD turns his face against those who do evil; he will erase their memory from the earth.

PSALM 34:11-16 NLT

. . . .

Heavenly Father, help me to constantly turn away from evil and sin. Because Your Son offered me the way to be Your child, I know that You will always be my Father—no matter what. But I know that sin in my life can have negative effects on our relationship and our communication. I always want to be in close fellowship with You, dear Father. Forgive me for my sin. Please cover it with Your amazing grace. Thank You, my God and Savior! Amen.

I WILL YET PRAISE HIM

Why, my soul, are you downcast? Why so disturbed within me? Put your hope in God, for I will yet praise him, my Savior and my God.

PSALM 42:11 NIV

Dear heavenly Father, my dream is crushed. My heart is broken. My disappointment wells up inside and shows itself through tears. I am so distressed. And yet, in moments of clarity, I can see that even now You are God and You are in control. I will praise You even now. For You are my Savior. You are my God. You are my Rock and Redeemer, and You hold all things together. My current situation is not a mistake. It is not beyond You, Father. You can take this time of sorrow and use it to grow a stronger me. New doors will open where old ones have slammed shut. New opportunities will spring forth in my life. You will put them there in my path. I trust You, God. Even in this time of loss and grief for what I thought might be. I give it all to You in Jesus' name. Amen.

GOD IS STILL THERE

Whoever dwells in the shelter of the Most High will rest in the shadow of the Almighty. I will say of the LORD, "He is my refuge and my fortress, my God, in whom I trust." Surely he will save you from the fowler's snare and from the deadly pestilence.

PSALM 91:1–3 NIV

. . . .

God, I know You haven't left me or even looked away for one moment. You are the same yesterday, today, and forever. That brings me great comfort, because right now I feel like my world has been turned upside down. I am so disappointed. I am struggling, God. I refuse to crumble at this trial. I will instead call out to You, my God. I reside in the shelter of Your presence. I rest now in Your shadow. You are my Refuge, my Hiding Place, a Fortress that protects me. I will place my trust in You. Set my sights on whatever is next. Take from me my past with its disappointment and provide a new dream for me to hold on to, I pray. In Jesus' name, I pray. Amen.

GOD HEARS MY CRY FOR HELP

When the righteous cry for help, the LORD hears and delivers them out of all their troubles. The LORD is near to the brokenhearted and saves the crushed in spirit. Many are the afflictions of the righteous, but the LORD delivers him out of them all.

PSALM 34:17–19 ESV

. . . .

Thank You, heavenly Father, for hearing me when I cry. Things are tough lately, and I am so discouraged. I know that You are near to me. I see You in nature as the sun continues to rise and set, even when I am so disheartened. You save the crushed in spirit. You deliver Your own out of afflictions. Please see my hurt and heal my brokenness. Put me back together so that once again I can feel whole. I will serve You all my days. Some days are just harder than others; I struggle to get out of bed and face the world. Help me today, Lord. Give me strength. Remind me that even in my distress, You have not forgotten me. You will see me through, and even this shall pass. In Jesus' name, I pray. Amen.

TRIALS ARE GIFTS

*Consider it a sheer gift, friends, when tests and
challenges come at you from all sides. You know
that under pressure, your faith-life is forced
into the open and shows its true colors. So
don't try to get out of anything prematurely.
Let it do its work so you become mature and
well-developed, not deficient in any way.*

JAMES 1:2–4 MSG

God, strengthen my faith in this time of difficulty, I
pray. Walk with me. Take me *through* it, even though
it would be so much easier to find a shortcut *around*
it. I know that when we come out on the other side
of this roadblock, You will have strengthened my
faith through the experience. So while I cannot say
I am excited about facing it, I will rejoice even in
this trial. I know it will be for my good in the long
run. Thank You for assuring me that You will be with
me. I am ready to tackle this challenge with You—we
can do it together! In Jesus' name. Amen.

HOLY ARMOR

We are not fighting against flesh-and-blood enemies, but against evil rulers and authorities of the unseen world, against mighty powers in this dark world, and against evil spirits in the heavenly places. Therefore, put on every piece of God's armor so you will be able to resist the enemy in the time of evil. Then after the battle you will still be standing firm. Stand your ground, putting on the belt of truth and the body armor of God's righteousness. For shoes, put on the peace that comes from the Good News so that you will be fully prepared. In addition to all of these, hold up the shield of faith to stop the fiery arrows of the devil. Put on salvation as your helmet, and take the sword of the Spirit, which is the word of God.

EPHESIANS 6:12–17 NLT

Heavenly Father, please remind me every day that spiritual battle is a real thing. Unseen enemy forces are trying to fight against every good thing You do. They attack Your people, trying to destroy them, and they try to keep people from turning away from sin and accepting You as Savior. Prepare me each day with Your holy armor to stand firm and fight against this evil, I pray. Amen.

WALK BY FAITH

For we walk by faith, not by sight.
2 CORINTHIANS 5:7 ESV

Dear Jesus, I will face difficulty head-on and won't back down. I will remember all You have shown me in the light while I walk through the darkness. You have revealed to me that You are the Son of God. You are the Messiah sent to save us from our sins. You promise us abundant life here on earth, and eternal life with You in heaven when we die. I have much to look forward to! Thank You, Lord Jesus, that I do not walk alone. Thank You that I do not walk only according to what I can see, because frankly, at times I can't see more than one step ahead. Give me the grace to walk in the light that I have been given for this day. Help me, Jesus, to walk by faith. In Your name, I pray. Amen.

EVERLASTING GOD

Have you not known? Have you not heard? The
LORD is the everlasting God, the Creator of the ends
of the earth. He does not faint or grow weary; his
understanding is unsearchable. He gives power to
the faint, and to him who has no might he increases
strength. Even youths shall faint and be weary,
and young men shall fall exhausted; but they who
wait for the LORD shall renew their strength; they
shall mount up with wings like eagles; they shall run
and not be weary; they shall walk and not faint.

ISAIAH 40:28–31 ESV

God, I may be only the created, but I am made in
the image of my Creator. I bear Your signature as
Your created masterpiece. Even on my darkest day,
this little light of mine still shines. Today I need Your
strength, Father. I cannot do life on my own. Remind
me of that timeless truth, that forever promise that
I will run and not grow weary, I will walk and not
faint. Help me to mount up with wings like eagles
and soar. In Jesus' name, I pray. Amen.

GOD'S MERCIES ARE
NEW EVERY DAY

But I will sing of your strength, in the morning
I will sing of your love; for you are my
fortress, my refuge in times of trouble.

PSALM 59:16 NIV

. . . .

God, Your mercies are new every morning. Each day You give me a clean slate. I wake up singing of Your love. It envelops me and reminds me that I am not the sum of what I have done. I am saved by the blood of Jesus. I am not my past; I am Your child. My past mistakes do not define me. I am ready to begin anew. You are my Fortress. You take care of me in times of trouble. When I am tempted to return to my old ways, You remind me of the blessings of walking with You. When I turn to look over my shoulder, You take my hand and lead me forward into the bright future You have planned for me. Because of You, Father, my future will be better than my past. Jesus makes all the difference in the world. In His name, I pray. Amen.

FORGETTING THE PAST

Brothers and sisters, I do not consider myself yet to have taken hold of it. But one thing I do: Forgetting what is behind and straining toward what is ahead, I press on toward the goal to win the prize for which God has called me heavenward in Christ Jesus.

PHILIPPIANS 3:13–14 NIV

Heavenly Father, help me to truly forget what is behind and strain toward what is ahead. It's hard to close the door on what has happened in the past. It seeps back into my memories and sometimes in my dreams. I try to take every thought captive to Christ, but some days it is easier to do than others. As I seek to press on toward the goal, remind me daily that You are with me. I need You by my side in order to truly lay aside the negative and run toward the positive. I am so blessed in my new life to be walking with Jesus. Please help me to never return to my old sin nature. In Jesus' name, I pray. Amen.

NEW LIFE IN CHRIST

*"I have been crucified with Christ and I no longer
live, but Christ lives in me. The life I now live in the
body, I live by faith in the Son of God, who loved
me and gave himself for me. I do not set aside
the grace of God, for if righteousness could be
gained through the law, Christ died for nothing!"*

GALATIANS 2:20–21 NIV

Dear God, it's truly a miracle. New life. I have been
born again. Nicodemus didn't understand this concept. He thought Jesus meant that a man would
truly be born of his mother's womb a second time.
However, I understand the concept and even beyond that, I have experienced it. A spiritual rebirth.
A second chance. A new lease on life. I thank You
that my old life died and that I was raised to a new
life. The old me is now dead. I stand here a new
woman. I will live by faith in Christ, who made this
new life possible for me. In His precious name, I
pray. Amen.

HID IN MY HEART

I have hidden your word in my heart, that I might not sin against you. I praise you, O LORD; teach me your decrees. I have recited aloud all the regulations you have given us. I have rejoiced in your laws as much as in riches. I will study your commandments and reflect on your ways. I will delight in your decrees and not forget your word. Be good to your servant, that I may live and obey your word. Open my eyes to see the wonderful truths in your instructions.

PSALM 119:11–18 NLT

. . . .

Heavenly Father, as I read Your Word and listen to teachings of Your Word, please help what I'm learning to stick in my mind and in my heart. Help me recall scripture exactly when I need it. I want to use it to keep me from sinning against You. I want to love and obey all You have said in Your Word and live it out to help others know and love You too. Amen.

HE FORGETS MY PAST SIN

Do not remember the sins of my youth and my rebellious ways; according to your love remember me, for you, LORD, are good.

PSALM 25:7 NIV

Dear heavenly Father, I know that You tell me You have forgotten my sin. So why do I keep reminding You of it? I see the consequences of my past sin; I am living out those consequences. I know that things would be different had I made better choices. But I hear You whisper over me that You will work all things together for good. You can create beauty from messes. You did it in the life of Saul, who became Paul. You used tax collectors and prostitutes for Your purposes, Father God. You see us as righteous once we are saved. You see me through a Jesus lens. Everything that was in my past, You have graciously left there. Now help me to do the same so that I may find peace, Father. I ask that You would remind me of Your goodness and of Your unfailing love for me. In Jesus' name, I pray. Amen.

BLESSINGS OF THE PRESENT

Don't ask, "Why was life better in the 'good old days'?" It is not wise to ask such questions.
ECCLESIASTES 7:10 NCV

• •

God, I look back on the past, and I have such fond memories. I dwell there when I should live in the present. Regardless of how great the past was, there were issues and struggles there also. We often look back with rose-colored glasses, remembering what we want to remember. Every season has its joys and its sorrows. There is not one that is better than another. Times are different. One season of life may bring more trials than another, but in every season, You are with me. You know the plans You have for me. You use the circumstances I find myself in to teach me and use me and grow me. I am blessed, Father. Thank You for my memories. Some of them are so sweet. But please help me move me forward. I don't want to dwell in the past and miss what You have for me today. In Jesus' name, I pray. Amen.

NO MORE TEARS

*"He will wipe away every tear from their eyes,
and there will be no more death, sadness, crying,
or pain, because all the old ways are gone."*

REVELATION 21:4 NCV

· ·

Heavenly Father, one day I will go to heaven. I will
enter paradise where there are no more tears. There
is no such thing as grief where You are, Father. There
is no disease or pain. There is no cancer. There are no
hospitals or surgeries, because everyone in heaven
is given a new body that has been made perfect.
On my darkest days when grief will not let up, I
rest in the knowledge that one day everything will
be made right. I look forward to that, God. I find
peace in knowing this life is not all there is for me.
One day there will truly be no more tears. In Jesus'
name, I pray. Amen.

JESUS DESTROYED DEATH

*But it is now shown to us by the coming of
our Savior Christ Jesus. He destroyed death,
and through the Good News he showed us the
way to have life that cannot be destroyed.*

2 TIMOTHY 1:10 NCV

. . . .

Heavenly Father, I am so thankful that Jesus defeated
death. The sting of death has no more power in the
life of a Christian. When death comes, we simply
pass over into eternity with You in heaven. We trade
a human existence for a spiritual one in paradise.
Grief is for those left behind because we miss our
loved ones. But for our loved ones who have passed
who know Jesus, there is no more pain for them.
There is only victory. There is only joy. They have a
new body that is so different from the earthly one
they left behind. Father, Jesus has made a way for
me to have an abundant life here on earth, and I
thank You that He has also gone to prepare a place
for me in heaven. Thank You, Father. In Jesus' name,
I pray. Amen.

COMFORTING OTHERS WHO GRIEVE

Blessed be the God and Father of our Lord Jesus Christ, the Father of mercies and God of all comfort, who comforts us in all our affliction, so that we may be able to comfort those who are in any affliction, with the comfort with which we ourselves are comforted by God. For as we share abundantly in Christ's sufferings, so through Christ we share abundantly in comfort too. If we are afflicted, it is for your comfort and salvation; and if we are comforted, it is for your comfort, which you experience when you patiently endure the same sufferings that we suffer. Our hope for you is unshaken, for we know that as you share in our sufferings, you will also share in our comfort.

2 CORINTHIANS 1:3–7 ESV

God, help me to comfort those who grieve. Please use me to be a hug or a shoulder to cry on as needed. Please show me tangible ways to help. Blessed are those who mourn. They shall be comforted. In Jesus' name, I pray. Amen.

OVERFLOWING PEACE

"Peace I leave with you; my peace I give you. I do not give to you as the world gives. Do not let your hearts be troubled and do not be afraid."

JOHN 14:27 NIV

Heavenly Father, my days are full, sometimes to the point of overflowing and chaotic. As I take a deep breath and begin this new day in prayer with You, please fill me with Your peace. Give me wisdom to create order in my life and to create space to breathe and think and especially focus on You. Guide me in the good works You want me to do, and direct me to the people You want me to serve. Amen.

IN CHRIST, I CAN DO ALL THINGS

I can do all things through him who strengthens me.

PHILIPPIANS 4:13 ESV

. . . .

I can do all things, Lord, through You. You strengthen me. You lift me up when I feel I can't go on. How I need You to carry me today. Grief zaps my energy. I find it hard to concentrate. My mind drifts. My heart aches. Every little thing around me reminds me of the past and of my loved one who has passed. I must rely on Your strength, for I truly have no resources of my own. Because Christ lives in my heart, I can press on. I will lie down and rest in peace; and when I awake, I will find enough power to face another day. I will take it one day at a time. I know that in due time I will be stronger and back to my old self. I love You, Lord, and I thank You for strengthening me in times like this. In Jesus' name, I pray. Amen.

FAITH IN GOD, NOT MAN

That your faith might not rest in the wisdom
of men but in the power of God.

1 CORINTHIANS 2:5 ESV

. . . .

God, I am often tempted to place my faith in men instead of where it belongs—in You. I trust in those around me and almost make them my gods at times. Certainly I want to please my employer, but he or she is not my God. I hope I can trust friends and family members, but my ultimate trust must be in my Lord. Give me discernment, Father, to see when I am trusting too greatly in man and not enough in You. I love You, Lord, and I have placed my faith in You. I am saved by grace through faith in Jesus, and I want to have a greater, stronger faith. You have come through for me again and again. Teach me to build altars at these places where You have blessed me. I want to live by faith, knowing that You will always come through for me. In Jesus' name, I pray. Amen.

FAITH IN JESUS

"Truly, truly, I say to you, whoever
believes has eternal life."

JOHN 6:47 ESV

· ·

Heavenly Father, so many people say they "believe," but they don't believe in You. Some have faith in themselves. They believe that they are strong. They don't see that they are weak and that only through You are they able to be strengthened. Some believe in many gods. These are lowercase *g* gods. They are not gods at all, in reality. Some believe in people. They make movie stars and employers and boyfriends their gods. They seek approval from these people. They long to be like them. They follow hard after empty pursuits. God, I am so thankful that the object of my faith is Jesus Christ. He died upon the cross for me—a horrible death. He bore my sins and the sins of the whole world that day. He opened up a path for me to come before You, a holy God. He is the Way, the Truth, and the Life. No one comes to the Father but through Jesus. Thank You for my faith that promises me eternal life. In Jesus' name, I pray. Amen.

GOD IS FAITHFUL

But he was in the stern, asleep on the cushion. And they woke him and said to him, "Teacher, do you not care that we are perishing?" And he awoke and rebuked the wind and said to the sea, "Peace! Be still!" And the wind ceased, and there was a great calm. He said to them, "Why are you so afraid? Have you still no faith?" And they were filled with great fear and said to one another, "Who then is this, that even the wind and the sea obey him?"

MARK 4:38–41 ESV

. . . .

Heavenly Father, I can read the scriptures and learn of all the times You proved Yourself powerful. I watch the Red Sea's waters part. I see Noah and his family saved from the flood inside the giant ark. I hear the baby's cry—a baby born to old parents, Abraham and Sarah. A promise fulfilled. You are faithful. You have great power. I know this. And yet, I still doubt. Give me greater faith, I pray. I am comforted to know I serve a God who always comes through. In Jesus' name, I pray. Amen.

LOVE GOD

And he answered, "You shall love the Lord your God with all your heart and with all your soul and with all your strength and with all your mind, and your neighbor as yourself."

LUKE 10:27 ESV

. . . .

God, regardless of my circumstances, I am called to love You with all my heart, soul, strength, and mind. I am called to love my neighbor as myself. So in times of rejoicing and victory, Lord, I will love You. And in times of want, I will love You just as much. I don't want my faith to be swayed by the winds of change. No matter where I find myself, may I always be found faithful. Help me not to focus on the outward circumstances but instead, help me see You in everything. May my love for You be evident to all those who know me. I love You, God. In Jesus' name, I pray. Amen.

CONSTANT PRAISE

Come, let us sing to the Lord! Let us shout joyfully to the Rock of our salvation. Let us come to him with thanksgiving. Let us sing psalms of praise to him. For the Lord is a great God, a great King above all gods. He holds in his hands the depths of the earth and the mightiest mountains. The sea belongs to him, for he made it. His hands formed the dry land, too.

PSALM 95:1–5 NLT

. . . .

Heavenly Father, I want songs of worship to You to always fill my mind. When I am in pain, help me to praise You. When I'm worried, help me to worship You. When I'm scared, help me to sing to You. No matter my need or the struggle I'm facing, or whatever blessing I'm receiving, I can cry out to You with requests, with thanksgiving, and with praise. May my words of honor and glory to You constantly overflow. Amen.

GOD WILL SHOW UP

But as for me, I am poor and needy; may the Lord think of me. You are my help and my deliverer; you are my God, do not delay.

PSALM 40:17 NIV

God, You are never too early, and You are never too late. My circumstances are not great right now, and I need Your help. I need to be delivered by Your hand. Provide for me, I pray. Remember my family, I ask. I know that You are aware of our needs. Please show up at just the right time. Please alter our circumstances. Do not delay. So many times in the past, I have needed You in other ways. I need You to show up again, God. You are greater than these circumstances. You are stronger. You are higher. In the power of Jesus' name, I pray. Amen.

PEACE IN ANY CIRCUMSTANCE

Great peace have those who love your law,
and nothing can make them stumble.

PSALM 119:165 NIV

. . . .

Heavenly Father, I love You. I love Your Word. It is a light unto my path. It sheds light into the dark recesses of my mind. It gives instruction and correction. It comforts and guides. I love Your law. I seek to obey Your commands and walk in Your ways. I know that when I do so, my life is filled with peace, regardless of my outward circumstances. You assure me that in this world I will find trouble. But I will continue to love You. I will continue to read and meditate upon Your law. I will walk in Your ways and seek to do Your will all the days of my life. Nothing can make me stumble if this is true. Nothing. No illness. No sorrow. No disappointment or loss. No set of circumstances has the power to steal my joy unless I allow it. I choose joy. I choose Jesus. I choose life. In the name of Christ, I pray. Amen.

THE PROMISE OF ETERNITY

"I know that my redeemer lives, and that in the end he will stand on the earth. And after my skin has been destroyed, yet in my flesh I will see God; I myself will see him with my own eyes—I, and not another. How my heart yearns within me!"

JOB 19:25–27 NIV

. . . .

God, Job was a faithful servant. He endured so many trials and tribulations, but he remained true to his faith. I don't know how he did it, but I pray for faith like Job's. I pray that in any circumstance, I will remain true to You. Regardless of how bad it gets, I have the hope of heaven. I have the hope of life beyond this earth. No matter what comes to me, I will be okay. I have a Redeemer who lives. I have the promise of eternity. So I will cling to my faith. I know that Jesus lives and that I will spend eternity with Him. In His name, I pray. Amen.

COMMITTING MY WORK TO GOD

*Commit your work to the Lord, and
your plans will be established.*

PROVERBS 16:3 ESV

• •

In my work, Lord, there are so many ladders to climb.
There are so many ways to get to the top. I don't
desire the easy way. I will take no shortcuts that
require me to be unethical. I believe that slow and
steady wins the race. I believe that doing things the
right way always pays off. I believe that if I commit
my aspirations to You, You will bless them. In Jesus'
name, I ask You to bless my work and help me to
reach my goals if it is Your will. Amen.

BLESSED,
AND A BLESSING

*Now the LORD said to Abram, "Go from your
country and your kindred and your father's
house to the land that I will show you. And I will
make of you a great nation, and I will bless you
and make your name great, so that you will be
a blessing. I will bless those who bless you, and
him who dishonors you I will curse, and in you
all the families of the earth shall be blessed."*

GENESIS 12:1–3 ESV

• •

God of Abraham, Isaac, and Jacob. . .God of my fore-
fathers. . .God, who is with me, who made me, who
sees me, who longs to bless me. I come before You.
I ask You to bless me and to help me be a blessing
to others. May I stand out as a servant leader, one
who is never too high up to take on a menial task.
May I look like Jesus in my workplace. I pray that if
You raise me up, I will always remember the One
who took me there. You alone deserve all honor
and glory and praise. In Jesus' name, I pray. Amen.

ENCOURAGED BY TRUTH

We know that all creation has been groaning as in the pains of childbirth right up to the present time. And we believers also groan, even though we have the Holy Spirit within us as a foretaste of future glory, for we long for our bodies to be released from sin and suffering. We, too, wait with eager hope for the day when God will give us our full rights as his adopted children, including the new bodies he has promised us. We were given this hope when we were saved. (If we already have something, we don't need to hope for it. But if we look forward to something we don't yet have, we must wait patiently and confidently.)

ROMANS 8:22–25 NLT

. . . .

Heavenly Father, sometimes it seems the only thing I can do is groan to You because I feel overwhelmed—by the needs of others around me, by needs of my own, and by the sin that touches everything in this world. Encourage me with the truth that all Your creation and all Your believers are groaning as we wait for You, but we do so with great hope and with Your Holy Spirit helping us. We trust You are working all things out for good for those of us who love You and are called to Your purpose. Amen.

GOD ESTABLISHES MY STEPS

In their hearts humans plan their course,
but the LORD establishes their steps.

PROVERBS 16:9 NIV

Heavenly Father, I have made my plans. I have set my goals. I know the direction I see myself going in my family life and my career. I recognize my gifts and abilities, and I have ideas of how to best use them for Your glory. But, that being said, I want to submit to Your will. You are the Master Planner. You are the One who establishes my steps regardless of the dreams I may have. Thank You, God, that I can trust You. You will never take me down a road that is not best for me. You know the plans You have for me, and they are for my good. I find great serenity in the knowledge that You, my God, are in control. In Jesus' name, I pray. Amen.

GROW MY FAITH

*And I am sure of this, that he who
began a good work in you will bring it to
completion at the day of Jesus Christ.*
PHILIPPIANS 1:6 ESV

. . . .

Heavenly Father, You have brought me so far. I want to continue to grow in my faith and to mature. I want to please You in all that I do. If my aspirations do not line up with Your good will for me, please change my dreams. Please plant in my heart the goals and desires that You want me to have. Make me open to whatever You have planned for me. I know that, far more important than exactly what career path I take, is the way You desire to mature me in my faith. Use me, God. Alter my dreams as You see fit. In Jesus' name, I pray. Amen.

IF THE LORD WILLS

Come now, you who say, "Today or tomorrow we will go into such and such a town and spend a year there and trade and make a profit"—yet you do not know what tomorrow will bring. What is your life? For you are a mist that appears for a little time and then vanishes. Instead you ought to say, "If the Lord wills, we will live and do this or that." As it is, you boast in your arrogance. All such boasting is evil. So whoever knows the right thing to do and fails to do it, for him it is sin.

JAMES 4:13–17 ESV

• •

Heavenly Father, I do not know what tomorrow will bring. This doesn't frighten me, though, because I know the One who holds tomorrow in His hands. Who am I to make plans? You are the Alpha and the Omega. The Beginning and the End. You were before all things; You are in all things; and You hold all things together. I ask You to remind me that all my plans should be filtered through Your loving fingers. In Jesus' name, I pray. Amen.

FAMILY AND FRIENDS

*God sets the lonely in families, he leads
out the prisoners with singing; but the
rebellious live in a sun-scorched land.*

PSALM 68:6 NIV

God, sometimes I feel lonely. Thank You for my family members who always have a way of lifting my spirits. Thank You also for friends who have become like family over the years. This world can be a cruel place. There are so many demands on me, and I feel stressed at times. But when I enter into a time of fellowship with my family and friends, all of that seems to disappear. You set the lonely in families. Thank You for the serenity I find when I am surrounded by my loved ones. Help me to be aware of those in my circles who may not have friends and family. Especially at the holidays, Lord, help me to be mindful of those who may experience loneliness. May there always be room in my home for one more to join us! In Jesus' name, I pray. Amen.

SERENITY IN SOLITUDE

But Jesus often withdrew to
lonely places and prayed.

LUKE 5:16 NIV

. . . .

Lord, while it is fun to be surrounded by friends, family, and colleagues, I need time to be alone as well. We all do. It is a time to recharge and rejuvenate. I need that downtime. With all the pressures of daily life and all the roles I balance as a woman, this is especially important. Whether it is a few moments I steal to myself before everyone else in the house is awake in the morning or a few moments before bedtime, I pray I will find quiet time each day with You. This is important to my spirit and to my growth as a believer. Give me time to reflect and draw close to You. Show me that it is important for me to sometimes be alone and read Your Word. There is serenity to be found in solitude. In Jesus' name, I pray. Amen.

THE LORD KEEPS ME SAFE

*In peace I will lie down and sleep, for you
alone, LORD, make me dwell in safety.*

PSALM 4:8 NIV

You alone, Lord, cause me to dwell in safety. You
look out for me. Just as a famous person or a leader
of a country walks always with a bodyguard at his or
her side, I walk with my God. You are never far away.
You neither sleep nor slumber. All the days of my
life I will walk with goodness and mercy following
me, because I belong to the Good Shepherd, the
great I Am, the sovereign God of the universe. I am
never truly alone because You are with me. I find
great peace in this. In Jesus' name, I pray. Amen.

CHOOSE FRIENDS WISELY

One who has unreliable friends soon comes to ruin, but there is a friend who sticks closer than a brother.

PROVERBS 18:24 NIV

• •

Lord, sometimes I look around and wish I had a lot of friends. I see people who seem to be so popular. Popular is not normally the way of the Christian, though. I can keep from being lonely by finding even one friend who sticks closer than a brother. Thank You for friendships like that. Thank You for blessing me with a few just as You had a few. I can love the world and be in it, but not of it. I don't have to be the center of attention or have a crowd of people around at all times in order to feel okay about myself. My security is not found in numbers. My security can only be found in You. Thank You for a close friend who loves me well. Help me to always have such a friend. In Your name, I pray. Amen.

COMFORT GIVER

Praise be to the God and Father of our Lord Jesus Christ, the Father of compassion and the God of all comfort, who comforts us in all our troubles, so that we can comfort those in any trouble with the comfort we ourselves receive from God.

2 CORINTHIANS 1:3-4 NIV

Heavenly Father, I praise and thank You for all Your compassion and comfort. You have shown them to me time and time again through so many different sources during every kind of suffering I've experienced. Remind me that You have comforted and cared for me so that I can in turn help comfort and care for others—and most of all point them to You as the Giver of it all. Amen.

GOD SEES THE LONELY

*A father to the fatherless, a defender of widows,
is God in his holy dwelling. God sets the lonely in
families, he leads out the prisoners with singing;
but the rebellious live in a sun-scorched land.*

PSALM 68:5–6 NIV

Heavenly Father, You fight for those who need someone to fight for them. You are sovereign and holy and yet, You are a God who reaches down to the lowliest of the lowly. Your own Son was born in a stable, laid in a manger for a bed. There was no room for Him in the inn. The world despised and rejected Him. They didn't recognize Him. But You saw Him. You didn't leave Him. When the time was right, He was lifted up. He returned to heaven and sits at Your right hand. You are a father to the fatherless, a defender of widows. You see us in our loneliness. Be with me now, I pray. Comfort me. Provide relationships for me that will fill up my lonely heart. Please bring serenity to my solitude, I pray. In Jesus' name, amen.

WISDOM FROM ABOVE

*But the wisdom from above is first pure, then
peaceable, gentle, open to reason, full of mercy
and good fruits, impartial and sincere.*

JAMES 3:17 ESV

. . . .

Your wisdom is true wisdom, God. So many people
scurry around here on earth. They think they
have found the keys to success. They promise
the same success to others. If you just buy this
product. . . If you just take this class. . . If you just
become part of this program. . . But these are
empty pursuits. They lead to nowhere fast. Your
wisdom shines. It stands out. It is different. It is
pure. There is no hint of the world in the wisdom
that flows down from heaven. It is gentle and
open to reason. It is not hotheaded or puffed up
with pride. It is not all about self. It is impartial
and sincere. There is nothing false or misleading
in true wisdom. Give me discernment, Father, as
I seek wisdom. Help me to find the peace that
comes with wisdom from above. In Jesus' name,
I pray for wisdom. Amen.

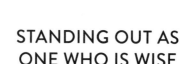

STANDING OUT AS ONE WHO IS WISE

Who is like the wise? And who knows the interpretation of a thing? A man's wisdom makes his face shine, and the hardness of his face is changed.

ECCLESIASTES 8:1 ESV

God, I want to stand out as a woman full of Your wisdom. There are people who have walked with You for a long time. I see them in my church and in my community, and I recognize them as Your saints. I see it in their eyes. They are not quick to make snap judgments. They are peaceful people, always ready to listen. They often listen more than they talk, but when they do share some advice, it is always very evidently godly advice. They are slow to speak, but their words bear great weight with those who will listen. God, I want to grow in wisdom. Please give me wisdom from above. Give me insight. Show me Your perspectives. Let me see people and events around me through Your lens rather than my own, which is so limited. In Jesus' name, I ask for wisdom. Amen.

AVOIDING FOOLISHNESS

*One who is wise is cautious and turns away
from evil, but a fool is reckless and careless.*

PROVERBS 14:16 ESV

Heavenly Father, help me to avoid the pitfalls Satan would love for me to fall into. Help me to be careful and to have wise judgment. There is more at stake than just my own life and my own welfare. The next generation watches me every day. They hear the words that spill from my lips. They take in my reactions to everyday life events. They will follow in my footsteps wherever I may lead them. My children will look a lot like me one day. Please keep me from being reckless and careless. Set a guard over my tongue that I might not sin in my anger. Keep my words pleasing to You. May my conversations be honorable and my word choice pure. Father, always set before me a glimpse into the future. Please bless me with the serenity found in wise choices. I pray these things in the name of the wisest One, Jesus. Amen.

A MASTERPIECE CREATED BY GOD

Thank you for making me so wonderfully complex!
Your workmanship is marvelous—how well I know it.

PSALM 139:14 NLT

. . . .

Heavenly Father, I often wish I weren't so complicated. Sometimes my feelings get hurt too easily . . .and I feel like I'm not talented enough at many things. But then I remember that to criticize myself is really an insult to You. You made me, and You created a masterpiece when You did. Mankind is Your greatest creation, Father. We are able to relate to You as our God. Help me to find peace with my identity in You. Even though I may need to gain or lose some weight. . .or get into better shape, help me to accept my body type and to praise You for it. Show Yourself strong in the areas where I know I am weak. This will point me even more clearly to You, Lord. If I could do it all on my own, I wouldn't need You as my sovereign God. I love You, Lord, and I thank You for making me to be me. In Jesus' name, I pray. Amen.

FROM DEATH TO LIFE

*We were therefore buried with him through
baptism into death in order that, just as Christ
was raised from the dead through the glory
of the Father, we too may live a new life.*

ROMANS 6:4 NIV

. . . .

God, I stand amazed that You would choose me as
Your own. I have been buried with Christ in baptism
and raised to walk in newness of life. Just as Nicodemus asked how in the world a man or woman could
be born again, so many are confused about this
miraculous gift of salvation. Our second, spiritual
"birth" is so much grander than our first. A physical
birth is a gift, but to be reborn spiritually is a far
greater one. I never have to look back on that old
life of mine again. I am a new creation in Jesus, and I
can walk and talk with Him as my Savior and Friend!
Just as Jesus died, my old life has passed away. Just
as He rose after three days, I have been raised as
His disciple. Thank You for new life. Thank You for
saving me! In Jesus' name, I pray. Amen.

RELATING TO MY PARENTS

*"Honor your father and your mother,
so that you may live long in the land
the LORD your God is giving you."*

EXODUS 20:12 NIV

God, please help me to honor my parents. Show me what honoring them means, now that I am a grown woman and they are growing older. I want to honor them in a way that pleases You, but sometimes there is strife in our relationship. I find it hard to balance all the roles I have now. I don't always make the same decisions for my life that they would choose for me, and yet I want to honor them. Teach me how to listen without being led to annoyance. Show me how to treat my parents with respect, no matter what. They are a blessing to me, chosen by You to be some of the closest people in my life. I love them, Father, and I want to honor You in how I relate to them. May this be a peaceful relationship for all of us. In Jesus' name, I ask it. Amen.

CONSTANT AND UNCHANGING

In the beginning you laid the foundations of the earth, and the heavens are the work of your hands. They will perish, but you remain; they will all wear out like a garment. Like clothing you will change them and they will be discarded. But you remain the same, and your years will never end.

PSALM 102:25–27 NIV

. . . .

Heavenly Father, when my world seems turned upside down with unexpected change, please give me comfort, peace, and strength by reminding me that You never change. You have always been and always will be, and You are always good. Nothing in my life is a guaranteed constant except for You, Father. Thank You for being my strong Rock of security. No matter what happens, I know You will never leave or forsake me. Amen.

MAKING A DIFFERENCE
IN MY WORK

*GOD took the Man and set him down in the Garden
of Eden to work the ground and keep it in order.*
GENESIS 2:15 MSG

. . . .

Father, show me relationships that I need to nurture
with certain coworkers so that, over time, I might
lead them to know Your Son as their personal Savior
too. As I work, give me endurance to accomplish the
tasks at hand. Give me peace with my colleagues—
those higher than me and those beneath me in rank.
May I find favor with my superiors even as Your
servant Joseph found favor in Pharaoh's palace.
Help me to speak up when I should and to hold my
tongue when that is what's best. It is in Jesus' name,
I pray, for You to guide me in my workplace. Amen.

WHEN WORK FEELS USELESS

I replied, "But my work seems so useless! I have spent my strength for nothing and to no purpose. Yet I leave it all in the Lord's hand; I will trust God for my reward."

ISAIAH 49:4 NLT

. . . .

Father God, my work wears me out, and it seems—at least some days—to serve no purpose. I don't always understand why You have kept me here in this job for so long. It feels like a dead end. I put in hours and hours, week after week, and for what? A paycheck that hardly covers the bills. Remind me that You have me in this job, at this time in my life, for a purpose. I may not always be here, but for as long as I am, please help me to honor You in it. Show me if and when it is time for a change. I pray that You will bring just the right people and job opportunities across my path when it's time for a change. In Jesus' name, I ask these things, and for Your glory. Amen.

PRAYING PROTECTION
OVER MY CHURCH

*But Saul was going everywhere to destroy the
church. He went from house to house, dragging out
both men and women to throw them into prison.*

ACTS 8:3 NLT

Heavenly Father, bring about in Your Church, a great
realization of the times in which we live. Guide us
to see that we must bond together and not be torn
apart. Nothing will destroy Your Church. You declare
that there will always be a remnant of Your people.
Let my church be one that pleases You in all we do,
and help us to live and worship and serve in harmony
with one another. In Jesus' name, I pray. Amen.

UNITY IN GOD'S CHURCH

*First, I hear that there are divisions
among you when you meet as a church,
and to some extent I believe it.*

1 CORINTHIANS 11:18 NLT

Heavenly Father, Your Church should not look like the world with all its strife and conflict. It should stand out as different. It should be a haven for people, not a place of hostility. May we come together as one body with one spirit. May we seek unity in the Lord Jesus above all else. Help us to major on the majors and not the minors. Help us to resist the urge to make mountains out of molehills. In times when we feel wronged, help us to come together and converse rather than assuming the worst about our brothers and sisters. Such amazing grace You have poured out on each of us! May we, in turn, show grace to each other. I know that we will experience great peace within our church when we choose unity over division. In Jesus' name, I pray. Amen.

TRUTH IN LOVE

Instead, we will speak the truth in love, growing
in every way more and more like Christ,
who is the head of his body, the church.

EPHESIANS 4:15 NLT

Heavenly Father, help my church and its leaders know how to speak the truth in love. Each situation is so unique, but help us to remember that they all involve people. And people are Your most precious creation, Your masterpieces that bear Your signature and image. Help us to value human life and to remember that it is often more fragile than it seems. There are times when correction must happen, but let it be done in love and with Your spirit. Help us to love all people and to realize that we too go astray. We are all sinners and lose sight of the right ways at times. I ask that we will be led always to speak the truth in love within my church. In this way we will grow more and more like Jesus, which is always our goal. In His name, I pray. Amen.

INSPIRED

*Anna, a prophet, was also there in the Temple.
She was the daughter of Phanuel from the tribe
of Asher, and she was very old. Her husband died
when they had been married only seven years. Then
she lived as a widow to the age of eighty-four. She
never left the Temple but stayed there day and
night, worshiping God with fasting and prayer.
She came along just as Simeon was talking with
Mary and Joseph, and she began praising God. She
talked about the child to everyone who had been
waiting expectantly for God to rescue Jerusalem.*

LUKE 2:36–38 NLT

Heavenly Father, I want the strong women of faith
featured in the Bible to inspire me. As I read about
Anna, I want to focus on how she suffered tragedy
but turned that into total devotion to You, staying
in the temple and worshipping You with fasting
and prayer. And then she was rewarded greatly
by getting to see baby Jesus and know He was the
expected Savior. If and when I suffer tragedy, please
help me to draw closer to You and know You better
like Anna did. Amen.

RENEW MY MIND

Do not conform to the pattern of this world,
but be transformed by the renewing of your mind.
Then you will be able to test and approve what
God's will is—his good, pleasing and perfect will.

ROMANS 12:2 NIV

. . . .

Renew my mind, heavenly Father, so that my thoughts might please You and my actions reflect Your great love. As a believer in Christ Jesus, just as believers who have gone before me, I must not conform to the ways of this world. The world calls out to do whatever feels good, to live in the moment, to think only about myself and what makes me happy. The world does not value You or Your ways, which are holy and righteous. Show me a different way, O Lord. Illuminate the path before me and shine Your light into the recesses of my mind. In those times when I am tempted to go the way of the world, draw me back, I pray. Train my mind and my heart to long for You and You alone. In Jesus' name, I pray. Amen.

THINKING OF OTHERS

*Don't be selfish; don't try to impress others.
Be humble, thinking of others as better than
yourselves. Don't look out only for your own
interests, but take an interest in others, too.*

PHILIPPIANS 2:3–4 NLT

God, please keep me from selfish thinking. Help me
to think of others before myself, never as less than
or not as important. In my humanity, I look out for
number one. But I am not a slave to my humanity
any longer. I have Christ in my heart. I am a new
creation. I can, in His power, look beyond myself and
my desires and even my needs. I can be proactive
in caring for those within my church community
and my workplace. I can move beyond the natural
to the supernatural. I can be "Jesus with skin on"
to those in need. I may be the only Jesus some will
ever see. Jesus was a servant leader on this earth.
May I follow in His footsteps. May I think of others
first. In Christ's name, I pray. Amen.

RESISTING SIN AS A RESULT OF ANGER

*"In your anger do not sin": Do not let the
sun go down while you are still angry,
and do not give the devil a foothold.*

EPHESIANS 4:26–27 NIV

. . . .

I get angry, Lord. I know I can't hide it from You.
You have seen it and heard it. You know all about
my emotions—even the ones that aren't so sweet.
The lesson You have for me in Ephesians is not that
I would never get angry; it's that I wouldn't sin as
a result of my anger. Tame my anger, Lord. Help
me to snuff it out while it's just a spark, before it
catches hold and becomes a wild and raging fire.
May I never sin in anger, Father. I love You, Lord,
and I want to please You. I know that You have the
power to defuse my anger before it gets out of
control. Please set a guard over my heart and mind,
that anger would not be a problem in my life. In
Jesus' name, amen.

ONE BODY, MANY PARTS

*Together you are the body of Christ, and
each one of you is a part of that body.*
1 CORINTHIANS 12:27 NCV

. . . .

God, help me to remember that while I am not
good at everything, I have been given gifts. And I
am to use them for Your glory. I will focus today on
my strengths, not my weaknesses. I will find ways
to use my talents to bring honor to Your name. I
am part of the body, and I play an important role
that no one else can play. There is a contemporary
Christian song that says it this way, and I dwell upon
these words today as I pray: "You are made to fill a
purpose that only you can fill, and there could never
be a more beautiful you!" In Jesus' name, I ask that
I would be aware of my gifts and that I will always
use them for Your kingdom, Lord. Amen.

DIFFERENT GIFTS

There are different kinds of gifts, but they are all from the same Spirit. There are different ways to serve but the same Lord to serve. And there are different ways that God works through people but the same God. God works in all of us in everything we do. Something from the Spirit can be seen in each person, for the common good.

1 CORINTHIANS 12:4–7 NCV

. . . .

God, in the wisdom and sovereignty of the Holy Ghost, it was determined that I would receive the gifts I have received. May I never question You or grumble about what I wish I could do instead. I want to live my life in service to You, God, and as a servant for Your people. May everything I do reflect this type of attitude. Thank You for the gifts You have blessed me with, and help me to recognize the responsibility that comes with my strengths and abilities. In Jesus' name, I pray. Amen.

TREASURES IN HEAVEN

"Do not store up for yourselves treasures on earth, where moths and vermin destroy, and where thieves break in and steal. But store up for yourselves treasures in heaven, where moths and vermin do not destroy, and where thieves do not break in and steal."

MATTHEW 6:19–20 NIV

. . . .

Heavenly Father, I pray that You would help me keep my priorities straight when it comes to my finances. I could work my life away sticking more money in the bank. I could save it all and hoard it for a rainy day, but that rainy day may never come. I can't take the cash with me to heaven. . .so help me instead to store up treasures in heaven. Help my real investments to be in people and relationships and service. Help my treasures to be time spent and scriptures shared. Help me to focus on heavenly things more than I worry about earthly ones. May my treasures always be stored up in heaven where they will be of eternal value. In Christ's name, I pray. Amen.

GOOD DISCIPLINE

And have you forgotten the encouraging words
God spoke to you as his children? He said, "My
child, don't make light of the LORD's discipline,
and don't give up when he corrects you. For the
LORD disciplines those he loves, and he punishes
each one he accepts as his child." As you endure
this divine discipline, remember that God is
treating you as his own children. Who ever heard
of a child who is never disciplined by its father?
If God doesn't discipline you as he does all of
his children, it means that you are illegitimate
and are not really his children at all. Since we
respected our earthly fathers who disciplined us,
shouldn't we submit even more to the discipline
of the Father of our spirits, and live forever?

HEBREWS 12:5–9 NLT

- -

Heavenly Father, please help me to appreciate the
good discipline You use to correct and guide me.
Remind me that You are always loving me perfectly,
even if I don't always enjoy what You're doing in my
life. Show me how You are shaping me and teaching
me and building character and endurance through
good discipline. I love You and want to grow more
like Jesus every day. Amen.

FINANCIAL PEACE

*Do not be one who shakes hands in pledge or puts
up security for debts; if you lack the means to pay,
your very bed will be snatched from under you.*

PROVERBS 22:26–27 NIV

. . . .

Heavenly Father, I pray for guidance in my financial
decisions. A debt-free life offers great peace and
serenity. Living under the burden of debt is never
fun. I know that in Your Word You say the only debt
that should remain between two people is the debt
of love. I should strive to owe nothing in regard
to money. Help me to find ways to become debt
free and stay that way so I will be free to be more
generous in my giving. Teach me Your principles,
Lord. Guide me to wise counsel who can help me
get a handle on my finances. I want this area of my
life to be aligned with Your statutes. I want to honor
You with my finances and find financial peace. In
Jesus' name, I pray. Amen.

A TIME FOR CHANGE

There is a time for everything, and a season
for every activity under the heavens.

ECCLESIASTES 3:1 NIV

. . . .

There is a time for everything, God. You make this so clear in Your Word. You created me. You know the plans You have for me. Every day that I will live has been ordained by You. Bear with me in my weakness, as change is always hard for me, Lord. Bring over me a peace that cannot be explained. Bring rest to my weary soul and help me—in this moment—to let go of the control. Help me to realize I serve a sovereign God who has not made a mistake nor has taken His hand off my life, even for a brief second. You are in this change, Lord. Help me to embrace it. In Jesus' name, I pray. Amen.

THE LORD FIGHTS FOR ME

The LORD gives me strength and a song. He has saved me. Shouts of joy and victory come from the tents of those who do right: "The LORD has done powerful things." The power of the LORD has won the victory; with his power the LORD has done mighty things.

PSALM 118:14–16 NCV

. . . .

Heavenly Father, I think of all the trials I have faced. You have walked through them with me—day by day. You have let me lean on You. Some days You have completely carried me. There are moments when I am so weak that all I can do is speak the name of Jesus. And in those times, I speak it boldly. You save me again and again, Father. Often, You are called upon to save me even from myself. And You always show up. You are victorious, Lord. I praise You now in advance for the victory I know You will provide in the face of yet another enemy. I am ready to go into battle with You, Father. In Jesus' name, I pray. Amen.

DISCOURAGED, BUT NOT IN DESPAIR

We are hard pressed on every side, but not crushed; perplexed, but not in despair; persecuted, but not abandoned; struck down, but not destroyed.

2 CORINTHIANS 4:8–9 NIV

· ·

Heavenly Father, thank You for being my Rock. You are there, and I instantly turn to You when I am in distress. Today I refuse to give up. I will not despair even in my disappointment. I will stand strong in my faith. I will trust in You. I may face persecution, but I will never be abandoned. I may fall down, but I will get up again in Your strength. I am not destroyed. I may have some battle scars, but I will be victorious. I have Christ in my heart, and I can do all things through Him who strengthens me. In His name, I pray. Amen.

RESIST THE DEVIL

Be sober-minded; be watchful. Your adversary the devil prowls around like a roaring lion, seeking someone to devour.

1 PETER 5:8 ESV

. . . .

Heavenly Father, I am struggling, but I am not destroyed. I will not fall prey to the evil one, who would love to see me give up on You. I find my hope in the living God. Satan would love for me to believe that this is the end of the road, that I should just give up. In him there is no hope; but in my God, there is *always* hope. Satan wants to tear me apart and devour me. He is like a lion in the jungle, just ready to pounce on its prey. Keep me ever watchful. Make me aware of his sneaky schemes. When I hear a message in my mind that tells me I am not strong enough, help me to stop right then and take that thought captive to Jesus. I am strong enough—not in and of myself—but through Christ, who gives me strength. I pray, in Jesus' name. Amen.

COMFORT IN THE LORD

"Blessed are those who mourn, for they shall be comforted."

MATTHEW 5:4 ESV

. . . .

God of all comfort, I come before You grief stricken. My heart hurts. I need You to reach down and fill me with supernatural peace. I find comfort when I read in Your Word that those who mourn are blessed, for they shall be comforted. As I speak the name of Jesus, I feel You near. I rest in the shadow of Your wing. I don't have the energy to question or even to cry any longer. I just rest here with You. I just allow You to hold me. I take in the comfort and the peace of knowing You. How could anyone face grief without You, Lord? How could anyone make it through a deep loss if there were not the hope of heaven on the other side? I love You, Lord. Thank You for comforting me in my time of grief. In Jesus' name, I pray. Amen.

ETERNAL REWARDS

"God blesses you when people mock you and persecute you and lie about you and say all sorts of evil things against you because you are my followers. Be happy about it! Be very glad! For a great reward awaits you in heaven. And remember, the ancient prophets were persecuted in the same way."

MATTHEW 5:11–12 NLT

. . . .

Heavenly Father, when I feel rejected, remind me how hated and rejected Your Son was—so rejected that people beat Him and then crucified Him. But thankfully that wasn't the end. In Christ's rejection and suffering You were working to offer eternal salvation. Remind me that You are working in ways I don't know yet when I am rejected and suffering too. Please comfort me and strengthen my faith as You work behind the scenes and prepare great rewards in heaven! Amen.

JESUS HEALS

*He heals the brokenhearted and
binds up their wounds.*

PSALM 147:3 ESV

. . . .

My heart is broken, Lord. I am so sad. In these quiet
moments with You, I find comfort in Your Word. I
read that You heal the brokenhearted. Could this
mean that You can heal me? Can You take the broken pieces of my heart and somehow put them
together again? I find peace in knowing that You
heal those whose hearts are broken, because that
is my condition in this grief. Bind up my wounds,
Lord Jesus. Nurse me back to a place of mental,
emotional, and physical health. I need You in these
days. I need You every hour. Be merciful with me,
I pray. Thank You for the comfort of knowing You
care and that You promise to take care of me. In
Your name, I pray. Amen.

FOCUS ON JESUS

*You will keep in perfect peace those whose minds
are steadfast, because they trust in you.*

ISAIAH 26:3 NIV

God of peace, meet me here. I am weary from my day, and I do not see relief in sight. I am tired, but I am not defeated. I find rest in You. I find comfort in knowing that You are God. I will fix my eyes on You. I know that You are mine and that I am Yours. I belong to You. You guide my steps. You know me, and You desire that I know You. I will read Your Word, and I will meet with You in prayer. I will not do all the talking because You have designed prayer as a two-way conversation. I will be still and know that You are God. I will listen for You in those moments. I will focus on Your ways. I know that there is great peace to be found for those whose hearts are steadfast. I desire such peace. In Jesus' name, I pray. Amen.

DO NOT BRAG
IN WISDOM

GOD's Message: "Don't let the wise brag of their wisdom. Don't let heroes brag of their exploits. Don't let the rich brag of their riches. If you brag, brag of this and this only: That you understand and know me. I'm GOD, and I act in loyal love. I do what's right and set things right and fair, and delight in those who do the same things. These are my trademarks." GOD's Decree.

JEREMIAH 9:23–24 MSG

. . . .

Lord, may I never brag about any wisdom that I gain, for it is all a gift from You. It comes straight from Your hand. May I boast only in You. You are good. You are loyal, and You act in love. You do what is right. You set things straight. One day every knee shall bow and every tongue confess that You are Lord. Until then, may I delight in the bits of wisdom You graciously bestow upon me. May I seek to be a bit more like You each day. The way of wisdom brings with it a refreshment to the soul. In Jesus' name, I pray. Amen.

WALKING WITH THE WISE

Walk with the wise and become wise, for a companion of fools suffers harm. Trouble pursues the sinner, but the righteous are rewarded with good things. A good person leaves an inheritance for their children's children, but a sinner's wealth is stored up for the righteous.

PROVERBS 13:20–22 NIV

• •

God, thank You for wise friends. Thank You for the relatives I have in my life who pursue wisdom and walk closely with You. Thank You for the Christian leaders in my circle. They lead me well in the way of wisdom. Father, I know that I could so easily be swept into friendships and acquaintances with some who would lead me down the wrong paths. Please provide for me wise and godly companions to do life with. Please allow me to walk with the wise so that I might also become wise. Provide godly counsel at times when it is needed in my life. Thank You for the peace that comes through walking with those who walk with You. In Jesus' name, I pray. Amen.

JOYFUL REGARDLESS OF CIRCUMSTANCES

Rejoice evermore. Pray without ceasing. In every thing give thanks: for this is the will of God in Christ Jesus concerning you.

1 THESSALONIANS 5:16–18 KJV

Lord, there are days when I can't help but rejoice in what You are doing. But many times the daily grind is just rather humdrum. There is nothing to rejoice about, much less give thanks for! Or is there? Help me, Father, to be joyful and thankful every day. Each day is a gift from You. Remind me of this truth today, and give me a joyful, thankful heart, I ask. Amen.

LISTEN AND OBEY

*"Go out and stand before me on the mountain,"
the LORD told him. And as Elijah stood there, the
LORD passed by, and a mighty windstorm hit the
mountain. It was such a terrible blast that the
rocks were torn loose, but the LORD was not in the
wind. After the wind there was an earthquake,
but the LORD was not in the earthquake. And after
the earthquake there was a fire, but the LORD was
not in the fire. And after the fire there was the
sound of a gentle whisper. When Elijah heard it,
he wrapped his face in his cloak and went out
and stood at the entrance of the cave. And a
voice said, "What are you doing here, Elijah?"*

1 KINGS 19:11–13 NLT

. . . .

Dear God, I pray to and praise You in multiple
ways and places, sometimes with spoken words,
sometimes just with my thoughts, sometimes with
singing, sometimes with written words. Help me to
remember that You speak to Your people through
anything You want, sometimes in big, dramatic ways
like the burning bush with Moses and sometimes
in quiet ways like a gentle whisper with Elijah. No
matter how You speak to me, Father, I want to be
listening for You and obeying You! Amen.

A GOD-CENTERED HOME

Except the Lord build the house, they labour in vain that build it: except the Lord keep the city, the watchman waketh but in vain.

PSALM 127:1 KJV

. . . .

Father, so many homes are shaken in these days. So many families are shattering to pieces around me. Protect my home, I pray. Protect my loved ones. Be the foundation of my home, strong and solid, consistent and wise. May every decision made here reflect Your principles. May those who visit this home and encounter this family be keenly aware of our uniqueness, because we serve the one true and almighty God. Amen.

REST IN THE LORD

Rest in the LORD, and wait patiently for him: fret not thyself because of him who prospereth in his way, because of the man who bringeth wicked devices to pass.

PSALM 37:7 KJV

. . . .

Heavenly Father, take my worries and burdens. I submit to You my anxieties. Fill me with the rest that calms my spirit when I trust in You. Sometimes I look at others' lives and compare them to my own. Why do they have what I desire? Especially when I know that they are not Christians! But You tell me not to be concerned with others' prosperity. I choose to rest in You. Amen.

RELAXATION

*There is nothing better for a man, than that he
should eat and drink, and that he should make his
soul enjoy good in his labour. This also I saw, that
it was from the hand of God. For who can eat,
or who else can hasten hereunto, more than I?*

ECCLESIASTES 2:24–25 KJV

. . . .

Thank You, God, for the gift of relaxation. It is so
nice to sit out on a patio in springtime or by the
fireplace in winter and enjoy a good meal with
friends or family. It is relaxing to my mind, my heart,
and my spirit. Help me to always set aside time to
fellowship with others and to relax. Thank You for
this blessing. Amen.

HIS RETURNING

But do not forget this one thing, dear friends: With the Lord a day is like a thousand years, and a thousand years are like a day. The Lord is not slow in keeping his promise, as some understand slowness. Instead he is patient with you, not wanting anyone to perish, but everyone to come to repentance. But the day of the Lord will come like a thief. The heavens will disappear with a roar; the elements will be destroyed by fire, and the earth and everything done in it will be laid bare. Since everything will be destroyed in this way, what kind of people ought you to be? You ought to live holy and godly lives as you look forward to the day of God and speed its coming.

2 PETER 3:8–12 NIV

Heavenly Father, I long for the day when Your Son returns and You establish the new heaven and earth where righteousness dwells forever. Remind me that You are never moving too slowly. You are so loving, Father. You want no one to perish but rather all to repent and accept Your Son as Savior. I praise You for Your goodness and patience, and I trust in Your perfect timing. Help me live my life to serve and honor You as I look forward to that glorious day of Your coming. Amen.

FINDING BALANCE

And, behold, there arose a great tempest
in the sea, insomuch that the ship was
covered with the waves: but he was asleep.
MATTHEW 8:24 KJV

. . . .

Jesus, when I think of Your ministry here on earth, I picture You teaching and casting out demons. You fed the five thousand and conversed with the woman at the well. You raised Lazarus from the dead! What a flurry of activity! But then I read that You slept. . .and during a storm that was frightening Your friends. If You rested, so shall I. I will set aside my work when it is appropriate to rest. Amen.

PATIENCE IN A BUSY WORLD

*Now we exhort you, brethren, warn them
that are unruly, comfort the feebleminded,
support the weak, be patient toward all men.*

1 THESSALONIANS 5:14 KJV

Father, patience isn't easy. This is a busy, fast-paced world in which I exist! I drive through fast-food restaurant windows and receive hot food within a few minutes. Automated bank tellers provide cash in an instant. There is not much I have to wait for in this modern age. But I realize that some of the things that matter most require great patience. Teach me to wait with grace. Amen.

MY STRENGTH
AND MY SONG

*The LORD is my strength and song, and he
is become my salvation: he is my God,
and I will prepare him an habitation; my
father's God, and I will exalt him.*

EXODUS 15:2 KJV

· ·

Lord, You don't just provide my strength. You *are*
my Strength. Through You, I am able to do all things.
At times I forget this. I lean on my own strength,
which is never enough. It always fails me. Today I
will stand firm on my foundation, which is salvation
through Christ. I will find my strength in the one
true God. I will worship You with my life. Amen.

REFLECTING GOD'S LOVE TO OTHERS

Having a good conscience; that, whereas
they speak evil of you, as of evildoers,
they may be ashamed that falsely accuse
your good conversation in Christ.

1 PETER 3:16 KJV

· ·

Lord, I truly want to influence my little corner of the world for Christ. Sometimes I can relate to the persecution that the heroes of the Bible experienced. It stings when someone sarcastically says, "Pray for me!" Help me to remember that I should never be ashamed of my faith. Give me a kind spirit and a gentleness that reflects Your love, regardless of the circumstances. Amen.

AVOIDING OVERCONFIDENCE

*Wherefore let him that thinketh he
standeth take heed lest he fall.*

1 CORINTHIANS 10:12 KJV

• •

God, it's easy to judge others. It's harder to take a
good look at my own life. I find myself thinking, *I
would never.* . .or *How could she?* What dangerous
thoughts! Where I am most confident that I would
never fail You, I just might. Your disciple Peter was
so sure he would not betray You and yet. . .look
what happened. "But for the grace of God go I"
should instead be my motto. Amen.

GOD'S COUNSEL
IS ETERNAL

There are many devices in a man's heart; nevertheless the counsel of the LORD, that shall stand.

PROVERBS 19:21 KJV

. . . .

Lord, I wish my heart was always in tune with Yours. I wish that I did not experience temptations to stray from Your perfect plan. But in truth, I struggle. There is a force within me that is fleshly and human. I feel pulled in the wrong direction at times. I know that Your counsel is eternal. It is a strong foundation on which I want to build my life. Strengthen me, I pray. Amen.

UNMERITED FAVOR

But we see Jesus, who was made a little lower than the angels for the suffering of death, crowned with glory and honour; that he by the grace of God should taste death for every man.

HEBREWS 2:9 KJV

· ·

Jesus, the word *grace* sounds so sweet. But when I think of You on that cross, bleeding, aching, dying an excruciating death, it takes on a new depth, a new meaning. You tasted death for me. You took my place. That is the grace of God. That is unmerited favor. That is unexplainable, unfathomable, and yet . . .true. Oh Jesus, thank You for Your grace. Thank You for dying for me. I will live for You. Amen.

LOVING MY ENEMIES

*For if ye love them which love you, what reward
have ye? do not even the publicans the same?
And if ye salute your brethren only, what do ye
more than others? do not even the publicans so?*

MATTHEW 5:46–47 KJV

. . . .

Lord, some of Your commands are easy to understand, such as taking care of widows and orphans.
But some of them go against human nature. It's
easier to show mercy to those we love, but You
tell us to love our enemies. You command us to
love those who are hard to love. Give me a love for
the unlovable, Father. I want to have a heart that
pleases You. Amen.

A TESTIMONY OF HOPE

But sanctify the Lord God in your hearts: and be ready always to give an answer to every man that asketh you a reason of the hope that is in you with meekness and fear.

1 PETER 3:15 KJV

• •

God, hopeful people stand out in a hopeless world. When others notice my ability to face trials without giving up, may I give a reason for it. That reason is You. Without my faith, I would be lost and without any hope. With it, I am able to maintain an inner joy even in the midst of tough situations. May my life be a testimony to the hope found only in Christ Jesus! Amen.

BETTER THAN LIFE

*Because thy lovingkindness is better
than life, my lips shall praise thee.*
PSALM 63:3 KJV

. . . .

I praise You, Father, for who You are! Your loving-kindness exceeds that of any human. You are good. You are beautiful. You are all things right and true. In You and through You, all things take their shape. This world is Your creation, and You choose to keep the earth turning on its axis. You bless us when we do not deserve blessing. Your love is better than life! Amen.

THE HOPE OF HEAVEN

In my Father's house are many mansions:
if it were not so, I would have told you.
I go to prepare a place for you.
JOHN 14:2 KJV

. . . .

God, I cannot even imagine heaven. But I know it will be a glorious place. I know that there will be no more tears there. You tell me that in Your Word. Even the sweetest worship of my God that I take part in on this earth is nothing like the worship there. Constantly, we will worship You, Father! You have prepared a place for me there. What hope I have in You. Amen.

SCRIPTURE INDEX

New Testament